Be a Successful Secretary
Philippa Ramage

A lighthearted philosophy for all secretaries and shorthand-typists with career ambitions

Pitman

PITMAN PUBLISHING LIMITED
128 Long Acre, London WC2E 9AN

A Longman Group Company

© Philippa Ramage 1982

First published in Great Britain 1982
Reprinted 1986

All rights reserved. No part of this publication may be reproduced,
stored in a retrieval system, or transmitted, in any form or by any
means, electronic, mechanical, photocopying, recording and/or
otherwise, without the prior written permission of the publishers.
This book may not be lent, resold, hired out or otherwise disposed of
by way of trade in any form of binding or cover other than that in
which it is published, without the prior consent of the publishers.

Text set in 10/11 pt Linotron 202 Ehrhardt, printed and bound in Great Britain
at The Bath Press, Avon

ISBN 0 273 01832 9

Contents

Preface v
Acknowledgments vii

1 **A review of the basic skills** 1
English 2
Shorthand and typewriting 3
Working with figures 4
Filing and record keeping 6

2 **Personal qualities** 15
Personality 15
Appearance 16
Your approach to the job 19

3 **Finding the job you want** 25
Deciding where to work 25
Where to look and how to succeed 29
Making a good start in a new job 42

4 **Communication** 51
Aiming for the best response 51
Organising what you need to say 51
Writing letters 53
Dealing with less pleasant people 58

5 **Responsibilities of your own** 61
Planning your day 61
Lightening your boss's workload 64
'Social' secretarial aspects 66
Report writing 68
Dealing with the Press 72
Recruitment of staff 74
Supervision, delegation and motivation 79

6 **Meetings** 84
Before the meeting: convening, agenda and preparation 84
During the meeting: the secretary's role 85
After the meeting: minutes, action list, and taking action 87
An example of a meeting 89

7 Travel 99
  Arranging and rearranging 99
  Itineraries and checklists 101
  Travelling for your company 105

8 Advancement 108
  Deciding when to move on 108
  Moving on with style 108

Preface

I believe that to get real satisfaction out of doing anything, you need to do it well. This book recommends some ways in which to improve your approach to working in a secretarial job; how to give more to it and so get more out of it. It has been written for the many talented young secretaries and shorthand-typists who, although having excellent basic skills, have not the experience or the confidence to know how to develop their careers.

I have not illustrated any forms, graphs, filing systems, furniture or layouts, since there are a myriad textbooks prescribed for college and business school courses which already do this. Nor have I gone into descriptions of the 'hardware' found in the modern office. The world of electronics – typewriters, word processors, reprography, telecommunications and personal computers – is developing so rapidly that any discussion of this evolution would be out of date before it is published. If your approach is right, you will be able to tackle any new system or electronic aid and win.

I have suggested a few ideas for building confidence (in yourself and in others); for developing enthusiasm about the quality of work done; for finding ways of giving more constructive support to your employer; for seeking and finding areas of 'own responsibility' that will help you to progress to more senior and rewarding jobs.

Working for a living need not be a 'necessary evil'. It can be an essential part of a satisfying life . . . and it should be fun!

PR 1982

Acknowledgments

I should like to thank my sons for their encouragement of my writing and cartoons, and the firm of Westlers for allowing me the time and facilities to complete the book.

Author's note

Throughout the book 'he' has been used to indicate the employer/boss, and 'she' for the secretary. These personal pronouns are reciprocal.

For Pauline Miller

1 A review of the basic skills

Being a secretary entails far more than being a good shorthand-typist – but you still have to be a good shorthand-typist! You also need to be proficient in the English language, be numerate and have an orderly approach to record keeping.

The real reason for needing to have excellent basic skills is so that you can forget about them! That may sound paradoxical, but if you are worried about your ability to read your shorthand notes, to type quickly and accurately when the pressure is on to meet a deadline, to keep accurate and orderly records or to find something quickly in your files, then these anxieties will get in the way of your activities in the wider scope of your job and will undoubtedly impede your promotion to the most senior posts.

Groundwork put in at the outset of your career may seem like hard grind for very little immediate return, but the effort will be

'Groundwork put in at the outset may seem like hard grind ...'

rewarded. It is the best investment you can make for your future career success; confidence in these skills will give you the right start for developing your abilities in the wider and more exciting role of executive secretary.

If you feel absolutely confident of your excellence in:

English language
Shorthand and typewriting
Working with figures
Filing and record keeping

leave out this first chapter and start with Chapter 2 Personal qualities.

English

Transcribing from shorthand, audio tapes and other people's handwriting puts the onus on you to be able to spell, punctuate and write grammatically. Since you have decided to be a secretary (and been interested enough to buy this book!), you probably enjoy reading and may like writing personal letters. This will be a good base for writing business letters and reports if you are asked to do so at work.

You will know where your shortcomings lie, but you may not be doing anything to overcome them. If, for instance, you feel less than confident about your ability to spell, then take active steps to improve. Correct spelling is certainly a basic necessity for being an executive secretary. Many extremely successful businessmen would fail a spelling test; they rely completely on their secretaries to correct their mistakes (as well as their sometimes inadequate grammar and choice of words).

Buy a good dictionary and, with its aid, set yourself to learn the spelling and definitions of five or ten words a day. Write at least one sentence using each of the words to help you remember its meaning. If you hear or read words you are unsure of, look them up in your dictionary, write them down and memorise them. It may sound a tedious occupation, but keep in mind that the English language has a remarkably comprehensive range, and the ability to choose exactly the right words to convey perfectly your intent is rare – and in legal matters it can be essential.

A thesaurus of synonyms and antonyms is a useful addition to your personal library. It will help to build your vocabulary so that when asked at work to write your own letters, reports or minutes, you will never be at a loss for the right word. There are also a number of books on the correct use of English which you can borrow from your public library to refresh your knowledge on correct grammar and good sentence construction.

Reading well written books, magazine and newspaper articles can show you how to write sentences that are easy to understand and well constructed. Reading material that is not so well written (but whose subject matter is interesting to you) can help to develop your critical powers; as a learning exercise you can rewrite certain passages to improve them.

At work you will be able to save your boss time and energy if he can rely on you to write an appropriate letter from his basic (and often cryptic) notes. For example, in reply to a letter requesting a donation to certain funds, he can simply write 'yes' and an amount or 'no', and from this you will write a suitable letter that the recipient will be glad to read – even if the answer is in the negative! (See Chapter 4 Communication).

Shorthand and typewriting

As a good secretary, your ability in these basic skills must be beyond reproach. Your shorthand and typewriting do not necessarily have to be particularly fast (although this will help) but they *must be accurate*. Try not to regard these skills as 'the boring part of the job'. Interest in a subject not only makes learning easier but makes it possible to become near-perfect which, in turn, gives one a real sense of satisfaction.

Learning shorthand is like learning a new language. Your vocabulary and speed in writing and reading it can grow with the years in a similar way to a knowledge of and expertise in a foreign language. Shorthand is also an art form; the more perfect your outlines, the easier they are to read. Developing a facility for writing outlines perfectly and fast is a real achievement.

There are many systems of shorthand and all have their particular merit. The Pitman New Era system has the widest scope and the possibility of attaining the highest speeds, but whatever form you learn make sure that you become an expert.

Very high speeds in shorthand writing are seldom called for in office work. Few people dictate for long periods at high speed; they may have the odd burst of speaking at 150 words a minute or faster, but it will only be for a few sentences. There will be pauses during dictation, or dictation at less than 50 words a minute, which enable you to catch up, provided you can write consistently and confidently at between 100 and 120 words a minute. The essential point is that you are always able to read what you have written, even if you have to leave it untranscribed for days.

As you progress to being secretary to more senior executives, you may find that less of your day will be taken up with writing and transcribing shorthand (and with typing). However, there will always be a certain amount of both, and once these skills have been learned correctly they are never forgotten. Your shorthand speed may decline, however, and it is worthwhile taking down and transcribing the occasional news report to keep in practice. The BBC's Overseas News Service is broadcast at excellent dictation speed. Reading magazines aimed at improving the shorthand writer's skills (such as *MEMO* and *Pitman 2000*) is also useful for maintaining your facility in the language and adding to your store of short forms and phrasing which will increase your speed. The journal *Office Skills*, although intended primarily for teachers, has many interesting and informative articles which will keep you up to date on new developments in the office world.[1]

While shorthand can be viewed as an 'art form', it can be difficult to see beyond the typewriter as a 'machine' and yourself, therefore, as a 'machine operator'. The aim of typing something is to provide easily read material quickly. The typist's function is to produce this copy accurately, speedily and attractively. It is no mean achievement to do this, and the way a page is set out – even if you use a word processor – is still the choice of the typist. If you try to visualise your typewriter (or word processor) as an 'instrument' rather than a machine, and yourself as a solo performer, you will see that typing can be an art form also. Think of yourself as a virtuoso, and each job becomes a 'performance' (or perhaps just a rehearsal if you are typing a draft). This can help you to enjoy becoming a fast, accurate and elegant typist.

Consider both the shorthand and typewriting functions of the secretary's role as having merit in their own right. By your attainment of real quality as a shorthand-typist you will have the best possible start in your career as an executive secretary.

Working with figures

Most secretarial jobs require numeracy. As with the use of words, so ability with figures is a skill acquired with practice. It is not a 'gift', and anyone can deal accurately with figures if sufficient effort and care are given.

If you are to be in charge of the petty cash or are responsible for keeping records of certain expenses or for paying your boss's personal accounts, some very simple bookkeeping will be called for. The books you keep will be straightforward but they must be specific and kept up to date.

Petty cash

The petty cash book will need details of the following:

The date of the transaction

---

[1] All three magazines are published by Pitman Periodicals Ltd, 128 Long Acre, London WC2E 9AN.

To or from whom the payment was made or received
The voucher (or receipt) number
The amount of the transaction (entered under the appropriate column)
Debit and credit columns (totalling entries on each line)

The Accounts staff will need all these details from your petty cash book when they come to enter them in their nominal accounts. In other words, if you enter your receipts and payments in columns headed with the various categories you deal with (for example, 'Postage', 'Stationery'), it will enable the Accountant to see clearly and quickly what your transactions have been and to note each item in the correct ledger.

Expense accounts

You may have to organise your boss's expense account claims. These will probably need to be entered on forms designed for this purpose and then submitted, together with invoices or receipts, to the Accounts Office or Chief Accountant at regular intervals for reimbursement.

Your greatest challenge here may be to persuade your boss not only to give you the relevant details of his expenses regularly, but to supply the receipts where applicable. If he will write down his expenses (possibly in his pocket diary) as they occur and pass this information to you, together with the invoice or receipt, as soon as you next see each other, the task is made easy. If he does not wish to do this, trying to recall how much he spent where, when and why can be a headache for you both, and possibly a financial loss for him. Give him a written reminder at frequent intervals to aid his memory, or, when you know he has taken business colleagues out to lunch, ask him for the receipt when he returns. When your boss has been away on a business trip, try to get him to sort through the various 'bits of paper' he has gathered while away and pass them to you on his return. If you both get into this routine it should never become a chore for either of you.

Personal accounts

Your boss may wish you to handle the payment of his personal accounts. He will give you a bundle of his unpaid bills once a month or will pass them to you as he receives them for you to keep until payment is due. Keep these demands loose in the front of a file marked 'Personal accounts'. After payment write 'paid' and the date and number of the cheque on the invoice, and then file it securely. Rule up a small notebook with columns headed: Date of account/invoice, Ref no, Amount, Payment to, Cheque no, Date paid, and keep this in the front of the file also.

Keep an eye on these accounts because it is possible that some of your boss's business expenses will come to his home address; you will need to identify these and include them on his expense account for reimbursement or pass them to the accounts office for payment by the company direct.

Accounting work

If you work for a very small company, part of your secretarial duties may be to undertake all the accounting (including wages and VAT records) supervised only by the company's external accounting firm (the auditors). You will be instructed by the accountant in the methods you must use, but to get a better picture of the accounting function borrow a few books from the library on the subject. Ask the accountant or your librarian to recommend some titles that will be suitable for a beginner.

If you take on a secretarial job where a substantial part of your work is with figures, it is essential that you decide at the outset when and how much time to set aside for these tasks. It is neither practical nor effective to 'fit them in' in odd moments here and there and to allow interruptions – even from your boss for that 'one quick memo' to be dictated and typed. You must allocate sufficient time to meet the deadlines for completion. Once you know how long various jobs take and when they are needed, set aside the appropriate periods and tell the people with whom you work when these periods are, requesting not to be interrupted except in a real emergency. Ask your boss to use his dictating machine or to make a handwritten note at such times, and to take and make his own telephone calls; this will be quite acceptable to him once you explain why this is necessary. Ask the switchboard operator to take messages for you during these periods and to put calls through to you only if they are really urgent. Of course, if you are also the receptionist/telephonist you will have real problems! Should the pressure be such that it is not possible for you to accomplish all the various tasks effectively, you will need to persuade the powers that be to engage some assistance for you as quickly as possible.

Filing and record keeping

The filing system

When you begin a new job, you may be lucky enough to inherit an understandable, well organised system that has been kept up to date. If so, all you need to do is familiarise yourself with it and follow the pattern set when adding to it.

If, on the other hand, the filing has been the 'poor relation' and relegated to the bottom of the priority list, then you will need to give a great deal of thought to reorganising it. This will not be possible for a while after beginning a new job because you will

'If the filing has been the "poor relation" and relegated to the bottom of the priority list ...'

not know enough about the company or the pattern of activities of your new boss and his department. You will need time to learn these things before you can be clear on how to go about setting up the most effective system. In the meantime, try to make sense of the way things have been filed in the past by reading through the files and continue with the existing format until you are sure enough to begin sorting things out. It is surprising how few really comprehensive – and comprehensible – filing systems there are to be found in businesses. To originate and operate such a system impresses everyone and saves so much time.

The purpose of a filing system
The purpose of a filing system is to:

a store documents in an order in which they can be easily located
b ensure their confidentiality
c ensure their safety and cleanliness

Ease of location Finding a document in the files quickly is essential to the smooth running of your job. A filing system is only efficient if *anyone* can locate things rapidly. There are many secretaries, excellent in other skills, who have devised systems so bewildering to others that no one else is able to find anything. This will not do. A system understandable to only one person is *not* a system. There are always times when the secretary is not available to find an item – holidays, absences while sick, or simply when someone wants a paper from the files and the secretary is not in her office.

A review of the basic skills

It is not practicable to set out hard and fast rules for the form your new system should take; it depends on the business and the needs of your particular job. Some large companies centralise the greater part of their filing and so you may have very few files under your direct control. Conversely, in a very small company, you may be the 'keeper' of all the company's files.

Indexing
An index of your system can simply be a typewritten list of names or subject headings in the order in which files can be found in the cabinets, but this means that when you add or take away from those files, the list needs retyping. There are a number of proprietary brands of file index that use an easily moved strip upon which the headings are typed. Better than these (if you want to keep more information than a strip will allow) are 'visible' indices where only the name is showing, but a card above it leaves plenty of room for further notes – address; names of people you deal with; when the company closes for specified holiday periods; if they have connections abroad; and so on, as needed. A small card index in a box on your desk can perform this function just as well, and these cards (or the visible index system) can double as your address book.

Ways to set up your filing system
Depending on the specific requirements of your department, there are a number of standard ways to set up your system:

- Alphabetical
- Geographical
- Subjective
- Numerical

Alphabetical Documents are filed under the first letter of the surname (or company name, or document heading), then by the subsequent letters in that name and, if necessary, by the accompanying initials preceding the name. Initials standing alone are usually filed first in an alphabetical system, as in the British Telecom directories. For example:

A Allan, Mr B J
   Allan, Miss W
   Allen, Rt Hon Trevor, MP
   Allison Company Ltd (The)

B Bright & Andrews Ltd
   Bugle, Mr A J
   Bugle, Mr A W

C CSS Limited
   Carter and Carter (Messrs)
   'Criteria for Management Action'

Notice that under 'C' a document has been filed under the initial letter of its title. This can happen if it is always referred to by its title and not called 'the paper produced by Webster', or whoever was responsible for writing it. If it is sometimes called by its title and sometimes by the name of its author, then you have the choice of keeping a copy filed under both initial letters or, if you have neither the space nor the inclination for copies, by 'cross reference' in your filing index. If you decide to file the paper under 'W', then your index under 'C' would read:

C CSS Limited
    Carter and Carter (Messrs)
    'Criteria for Management Action' (see Webster)

Geographical If you are in a company which has agents or salespeople allocated to different areas or districts, then filing under the location makes sense. For example, assume that the areas have been allocated as follows:

North Eastern	London and the Home Counties
North Western	Southern
Midlands	West Country
East Anglia	

Each of these seven areas may be further split by county, or between the various agents or salespeople dealing in that area, or both. The subsections within the geographical filing system will be shown by how the areas are divided and will simply be numbered or named files within that system. For example:

North Eastern Area: Depending on the size of the business, this could be one file or a complete drawer of files. The subdivisions might be:

District 1: Northumberland, Durham and Cleveland
District 2: North Yorkshire, North and South Humberside, and West Yorkshire

Within these subdivisions (again depending on the quantity of paperwork generated by each) there might be further subdivisions:

District 1.1 District Manager (Arthur McGillivray)
       1.2 Key Account Executive (Janice Brown)
       1.3 Salesperson (Sandra Kent)
       1.4 Salesperson (Michael Andover)

and similarly for District 2.

Subjective You may decide that the work you and your boss deal with falls clearly into various 'subjects', that you can define each of these and, where necessary, subdivide them as you choose –

geographically, chronologically, or in order of importance eg:

Design (main heading) sub-divided into:	Forward Plans Contracts Meetings Students and Colleges
Suppliers:	UK USA and Canada Europe Others
Manufacturing:	Subsidiaries Outside Contracts
Marketing and Sales:	Representatives/Agencies Retail Outlets – UK Retail Outlets – Overseas
Publicity and Public Relations:	Agencies Forward Plans Internal Memoranda
Administration:	Correspondence Finance Minutes of Meetings Reports and Memoranda

How many subdivisions you decide upon and whether you arrange alphabetically, geographically, in order of importance to your department, or in the timescale in which the activities take place (for example, designing comes before manufacturing and manufacturing before selling) will be a personal choice dictated by common sense. The example above is arbitrary and has been invented simply to show the kinds of heading and subheading you might find in, say, a small fashion trade business. It has been organised in order of timescale and to a certain extent also in order of importance and size of each operation as it touches the work of the department concerned.

Numerical This system allocates numbers to files as and when they are originated. It means that your index is vital as it is the only way of identifying a file. It must therefore be up to date and specific as to file content because all that is shown on the actual file is a number. When it is necessary to open a new file for a new contract, customer or subject, you will give it the next number in sequence and slot it into your cabinet behind the last allocated number.

Many centralised filing systems operate on the numerical principle and this is often sensible. However, it is the least attractive method for a personally operated system and has little to recommend it except confidentiality; it is impossible to determine by glancing at a row of files in a cabinet the subject matter they contain because, of course, all that is visible is the number allocated to each. To find the subject you also need access to the index. For example, the spine of a file might show 003478.1 while the index would read:

003478.1 Administration: Minutes and meeting reports from Sept 198– to Aug 198–

Confidentiality, safety and cleanliness Ensure that lockable cabinets are used and that all papers are filed promptly and regularly. Try to file papers at a convenient time each day so that the job never becomes onerous. This is for your own benefit because you will not be able to locate things easily if you let papers pile up in your filing tray. To have to search through many weeks' accumulated correspondence is no way to convince anyone that yours is an efficient system, not to mention the waste of time involved.

If your work load often makes it difficult for you to find the time regularly each day to file, try nevertheless to mark up each item with the name or number of its appropriate file and sort to the order in which they appear in your index (see below). The use of an expandable file (sometimes called a 'concertina' or 'elephant' file) with each compartment lettered or numbered means that you can mark up and sort papers to these compartments before depositing them in the correct files in the cabinets. If you have a junior available, once the items are marked up they can be put away by him or her. If you file or mark up every day, the job will take only a few minutes. If you leave it for a week it becomes a major task. Anything longer than a week and you will really have problems in finding things!

As an insurance you can operate a separate 'day file' where you keep an extra copy of everything you type. This is essential only if you type for more than one person or if your company operates a centralised filing system because, of course, you will not in these cases be in charge of the filing systems concerned and should have a record for yourself of what you have typed.

If you work only for one person, this file can still occasionally be of use. For example, if you operate an alphabetical filing system and you and your boss remember that you replied to a letter on a certain subject about a month ago but cannot remember the name of the writer, by looking through your extra-copy or 'day file', you can find a copy of your reply and from that be able to find the original letter in your main system. This extra copy file is also sometimes called an 'idiot file' for the obvious reason that one does not need to be very bright to find things in it. Be very sure, however, that this file is kept as confidentially as all your other files and not left out in your office available for anyone to look through.

The 'bring-forward' system
If you have written to someone with a query, it is obviously sensible to keep a note of this until an answer has been received. If papers need to be brought forward in due time for meetings,

conferences or travel, a reminder needs to be made of the date for retrieval. If you have a sufficiently large diary with space for these reminders, you can simply write in the appropriate instructions for action. An alternative is to use another expanding file (like the one referred to as an aid to sorting the general filing), with compartments numbered 1–31 and January to December.

It is wiser to put only *notes* of what is to be retrieved from the general system in this 'bring-forward' file and to keep the actual papers where they should be, since it is possible that they may be needed before the bring-forward date. However, if you do not have an appropriate file for the papers in your main system (perhaps because this is a 'one-off' situation) then you can put the documents themselves into the expanding file. For example: a meeting has been set up with a representative who has sent a brochure and samples of his company's services and goods in advance. You write the meeting date and time in your diary and put the brochure and samples into the compartment in the expanding file for that date. Note in the diary, and on your 'day file' copy of your reply if you keep one, where the brochure and samples can be found, in case you need the items in the interval.

File pruning
Find out how long it is necessary to keep papers in the current files in your office so that you can develop the habit of clearing out inactive papers by 'boxing' them for archival storage elsewhere. Over-stuffed files are difficult to handle and cabinets jammed tight make retrieving and replacing papers hard work. When a file grows too thick to be manageable, read through it to see if it can be pruned by 'boxing' or throwing away or, if this is not possible because the papers are all current, consider subdividing it in some way. You could perhaps have separate folders containing subsidiary matter inside the main file for the subject. For example, a file headed 'Association of Chemical Engineering' could have subdivisions for, say, 'Council meetings', 'Special committees', 'Newsletters' and so on. Having files subdivided in this way can save your time when looking for something; you will not need to search through a bulky 'general' file on the subject, but will have sorted into the various headings when you first set up the file. Don't carry this to the extreme so that you provide different folders for almost every bit of paper! Think about the volume of paper you acquire on any subject and allocate space sensibly.

Lending files or papers
Always make a note of files removed or papers taken from files. A piece of coloured card with the name, number or description of the folder or paper typed on it and inserted into the space from which it has been removed, giving the date of removal and by whom is a useful reminder. If files are regularly loaned to

others, keep a small notebook with headings for the name of the borrower, the reference for the file and 'out' and 'in' dates eg:

File description	Loaned to	Out	In
Allison & Co	J Wilkinson (Accounts)	4.7.8–	7.7.8–
Edwards Bros	Personnel	4.7.8–	
Suddard & Co	P Clark (Sales)	6.7.8–	8.7.8–

If you see from your list that a file has been out for more than a few days, follow it up and ask when it is likely to be returned.

Record keeping

The number of records, apart from the filing, that you keep will be indicated to you by your job description or by your boss himself. These will probably accord with systems already established and you will follow the pattern set. At first you will need only to be neat and orderly in your entries and keep all records up to date regularly and often. When you have been in the job for a while you may well decide that records could be kept differently and more efficiently, and in most companies sensible suggestions for improving systems are welcome. Make sure you discuss your suggestions with others concerned with these records before altering the way you do anything, just in case there are specific and valid reasons for *not* doing it another way.

Card index
The card index has already been mentioned as an aid to your filing system (a small box of loose or lightly attached cards which can be added to and removed easily). If you decide that this is not the best system for your filing index, then consider using it for your addresses and telephone numbers rather than a book which can rapidly become messy with crossings out and additions.

Graphs and charts
Another form of record keeping is to use a graph or chart to plot the pattern of particular facts or trends. These 'records' should, however, also be 'communicators', ie indicators of areas needing attention and guides to action-taking. It is thus essential that:

a their purpose is clearly defined
b they are well designed and up to date
c their usefulness is reviewed frequently by management and action taken

Purpose Well designed and current charts and graphs promote speed and clarity of communication – of past facts, present situations and possible future achievements. They can show at a glance a situation that could take a lengthy report supported by columns of statistics to describe. They can be used to present the state of the company's progress (or otherwise) in any field from research and development through to business ratios and corporate planning. Past trends are shown in perspective and realistic targets can be set.

Design The physical form charts take ranges from simple double axes drawn on graph paper with points plotted in different colours or configurations; through to bar, pie, flow charts etc; purpose-made wall boards with moveable plastic or magnetic indicators; or even sophisticated graphics programs on mini or mainframe computers linked to colour printers.

Action Make sure you understand the reasoning behind the information you receive and the figures you work on, and how these are to be interpreted, before you begin plotting them. If you are to be involved with 'charting' to any considerable extent, consult with your company's expert – or your friendly neighbourhood librarian again – for advice on suitable reading material to explain the mechanics of graphical presentation. It is a fascinating subject and the more you know, the better equipped you will be to enjoy this part of your job, spot errors when they occur and make a real contribution to the charts you draw up.

Never accept the task of updating a graph or chart whose purpose you do not fully understand, and do not continue to plot data on charts that nobody even looks at, let alone acts upon. Charts are only a management aid – a means to an end and not an end in themselves. Avoid the pitfall, quite common among dedicated 'chartists', of getting carried away by the sheer beauty of the graph, so that its purpose and results get lost along the way. If you want to draw pretty pictures or play games with the computer – take it up as a hobby!

Summary

- Improve your English language skill by reading and writing for your own pleasure; buy a good dictionary and reference books – and use them
- Master your shorthand and typewriting techniques; they must be good enough for you to forget about them and concentrate on the job content
- Familiarise yourself with basic bookkeeping principles by reading and learning from a simple textbook; keep your mind agile by using mental arithmetic; learn to use a calculator fully
- Give time and thought to organising your filing and record keeping to the best advantage; file and update records regularly and frequently
- Be certain you understand the purpose of the graphs and charts you keep; make sure they 'communicate' effectively

2 Personal qualities

It is a fact of life that an attractive person receives a better response than an unattractive one – but what is meant by 'attractive'? It simply means having the power to attract; in other words, having a balanced and appealing personality combined with a good appearance. Attraction encompasses the whole of you: how you look; how you react to situations; your interest in and response to other people.

How 'attractive' are you?
Make an appraisal of yourself, listing the good and bad points of your personality and appearance. Do you generally get on well with others or not? Are you interested in people? Are people interested in you? Are you ready to listen and help if asked? Do you get impatient with others' faults? Do you get impatient with your own faults?

Take a look in a full-length mirror. Do you look good? Well presented? Clean? Absolutely faultless – or a downright mess? If you feel you can risk the possible consequences, ask your best friend what he or she likes and dislikes most about you – then show them your appraisal and ask if they agree or disagree with what *you* think of yourself.

Personality

In order to develop your personality to its best advantage, you must believe in yourself and appreciate your good points. You need to make the most of the good and eliminate the bad. If you believe in yourself strongly enough, and work hard enough, you can achieve almost anything. If you feel diffident and lacking in confidence you put yourself at a disadvantage immediately. Don't let the thought of tackling something new frighten you. Never say you cannot do something, but rather that you will try. Most importantly, don't be ashamed of admitting to a mistake. One of the most disarming qualities in anyone is their readiness to admit they may have been wrong – or even that they definitely were wrong. Obviously you will never be a great success if you make so many mistakes that you are repeatedly having to say 'sorry, my fault', but confidence in your ability to do the right thing most of the time will enable you to admit to being in error with good grace when the occasion arises!

Open your mind to others. Look for their good points, especially in those not apparently gifted or immediately to your liking. You will so often find worthwhile qualities in anyone if you take the time to look. The art of listening is well worth cultivating; it is one of the best ways to learn – and to make friends. Always treat everyone with courtesy and kindness – even the aggressive salesman or the company bore. It usually takes less time and energy to be polite and caring than to be rude or indifferent.

Appearance

If you have been gifted with classic beauty as well as reasonable intelligence, then you start with an enormous advantage. All you need to do is concentrate on developing efficiency, tolerance and enthusiasm as well! However, since most of us are not 'beautiful' in the traffic-stopping way, we need to use all our efforts to make the best of what we have. Just as it is necessary to have self confidence in order to gain recognition, so you must believe that you are good to look at in order to persuade others that you are. Once you have opened up your mind, and presented yourself as one who cares about and considers other people, you are already well on the way to looking better. To smile rather than frown improves a face instantly. (It is not suggested you go about grinning like a Cheshire cat from morn to night, but a welcoming smile is much more attractive than a grim face.) With your pleasant personality and easy smile, you have improved your facial expression. With your developed interest in others, you have brought a new vivacity to yourself. This is an excellent base to build on in your quest for becoming really attractive.

Your daily bath or shower will be wasted if the clothes you put on are not absolutely clean. Pressure of work and your social life can mean that you find yourself rushed into snatching a sweater and skirt to wear that may be overdue at the cleaners. Plan in advance your 'working wardrobe' for the week and put clothes aside separately after wearing, for an inspection followed by any necessary washing or cleaning. Make time each week for regular sessions of sorting and cleaning. Take care of your shoes by regular polishing and repairing, and allocate the necessary time for hair washing, manicures and all the other small items of personal maintenance so essential to the consistently 'well-groomed' look.

Keep your make-up to a minimum; it is something you do not want to spend time on during the working day. Avoid really heavy perfumes for daytime use; cologne or eau de toilette is more appropriate and it is better to smell freshly of yourself rather than use an overpowering perfume which will be impossible for anyone to ignore.

What you eat can make a tremendous difference to the way you feel and look. A clear skin, good figure, sound, clean teeth, shining hair and eyes usually come from good health, the right diet and some outdoor exercise. Take a lunch of fruit, cheese or raw vegetables to work with you if these are not available in the cafeteria. The right sort of food can be more expensive than a short-order fry-up, but only superficially. Good food makes you feel better, look better and capable of harder work and clearer thinking. A well balanced diet and outdoor exercise (even if only a fast walk or jog instead of taking a bus or train for a few stops) will make you fitter and better able to resist infection. It makes sense to maintain the 'machine' which earns you your living and, if kept in good condition, adds to your abilities and enjoyment.

Choice of clothes The clothes you wear should be comfortable, attractive and in a style that you like. There is no 'secretarial uniform' as such, but certain companies do have preferences for what their staff wear – for example, the 'no jeans' rule still applies in many places. Try not to cause a sensation by whatever you decide to wear. Like your perfume, hair style and colour, and make-up, everything about you should be understated for the best effect.

The total impression

Study your face and figure in the mirror – critically but optimistically. Have you ever considered the total impression you give? Think, for instance, about how you stand and walk. Do you stoop? Do you slouch along, putting one foot in front of the other and never considering this as something that can add to or detract from your appearance? If you are not naturally graceful, don't accept that you are a 'clumsy oaf'; grace can be acquired. Watch your reflection in shop windows or mirrors as you walk down the street and notice whether you stand tall, hold your chin up and have an easy stride. No? Then try consciously to stand straighter, shorten (or lengthen, if you appear to be tottering along) your pace.

If you are tottering along, is it because you are wearing uncomfortable shoes? If so, discard them. It is important to wear comfortable shoes for working as you will probably spend a good part of your day standing and walking. Comfortable shoes are not necessarily dreary ones, but to find comfort *and* style you will have to take more time in buying them, and probably spend a little more money. Like a basic skill, shoes and their comfort are things you should take for granted and forget once acquired. If your feet hurt, you will not only walk badly; you will also put an unnecessary strain on your back and your discomfort will show in your expression. Be aware of your movements in all you do. Learn to sit down, stand up, hand someone a cup of coffee and do everything gracefully. It takes a real effort at first, but with practice it quickly becomes perfectly natural.

'... grace can be acquired.'

Your voice can be one of your greatest assets. An executive secretary spends a lot of her time talking, either face to face or over the telephone. Although it may sound silly to suggest that a smile can be 'seen' over miles of cable, it really can! If you smile when you answer your 'phone, you instantly impress the caller with your pleasant personality. He or she will feel at ease and able to talk freely to you. Even if you have a bad-tempered caller at the other end of the line, your smiling voice will very often put them in a better mood than when they started the call.

A very shrill voice is not desirable in a secretary, nor is a growl. Gentle, middle of the range tones are generally more attractive. If you have never heard your own voice as others hear it, make a tape and listen to what you sound like to others. If you can get a friend to tape your voice when you are unaware that this is being done, you will be more likely to hear what you really sound like, but if this is not possible, just read a passage from a newspaper or magazine in your natural voice on the office audio equipment if you have no tape recorder of your own. You can then decide whether you find your voice pleasant enough or whether it could do with a little improvement. It is not suggested that you put on a voice that is not your own; assumed accents and tone are not what you are searching for. But if you hear something you find unattractive in your own voice you can try to improve it. As with your appearance, there is an 'essence' which is you and which can be refined and developed.

The executive secretary is in the business of helpful communication and needs to present her whole person – looks, personality, approach and way of speaking – in the best possible way to encourage such communication between herself (as her company's representative) and the rest of the world she deals with. If she sounds like the 'dragon at the door' then no one in their right mind will want to speak to her. Develop your voice to express the best of yourself.

To your impeccable basic skills you have added a confident approach, good health, good looks, grace and a pleasant voice. You are immaculately turned out in whatever style you feel suits you best – and you have decided that for yourself, not by copying someone else (or even heeding the advice in this book). An independent spirit is just what you need in order to succeed. If your skills are excellent and you are a pleasant person, you will be able to look as eccentric as you please. How miserable and boring office life would be if all the secretaries looked and sounded as though they came off an assembly line, programmed to fall into just one acceptable category.

Your approach to the job

Aspects of your approach to your job are covered in the preceding part of this chapter and elsewhere in the book, but there are some specific extra qualities which are essential when you become an executive secretary/personal assistant to a senior member of the management team. Some of these qualities are suggested below, and although the list may appear formidable, if you have the first mentioned in reasonable degree, they can all be developed:

- Intelligence
- Dependability
- Confidentiality/loyalty/discretion
- Initiative/imagination/ingenuity
- Tolerance/ability to relate to people at all levels
- Willingness to learn
- Attention to detail
- Ability to work under pressure and cope with varying work loads
- Ability to adapt to changing situations
- Willingness to accept the 'collaborator's role' and not to seek or assume the power which belongs to your boss
- Resilience – the ability to accept setbacks and criticism
- A sense of humour

Dependability

This not only means that you can be relied upon to work late or arrive early if needed, but that tasks you are requested to carry out will be done without anyone having to remind you. Even if you believe you have an infallible memory, it is still a good idea to make lists for yourself of all the tasks you have undertaken to perform. A clip-board with a ruled pad is an easy way of doing this so that you can have your list to hand wherever you are. Keep on your desk a supply of message pads too, so that you can write down requests that come through you for your boss to contact someone or do something. You can also check your boss's reminder pad regularly to see that he is keeping up to date and whether there are any items on it that you can deal with for him.

Confidentiality/loyalty/discretion

You will be dealing with all kinds of private and personal information about the business and your boss and it is essential that you can be trusted absolutely. If you work for the Chairman or Managing Director there will be times when you are party to plans and data that not even the other board directors are aware of. Never leave papers on your desk when you leave your office and, if you are typing a confidential document when someone comes to talk to you, cover it with a plain piece of paper while they are in your office. Although some people can read from a great distance and read writing that is upside down, X-ray vision is so far unknown!

Your loyalty is firstly to your company and your boss – and you are the only one who can decide which takes precedence. Deciding this can put considerable strain on you in certain circumstances – fortunately rarely experienced. Your boss may be involved in activities which are dishonest or detrimental to the company and, if you are unable to persuade him to behave differently, you will have to decide whether your loyalty to the firm outweighs your loyalty to the man. On the other hand, where the firm – ie the other directors – are involved in dubious practices, and your boss finds himself unable to bring about a change because he is alone or in a minority in his views, he may decide he must resign. In either set of circumstances, probably the wisest course of action for you would be to seek employment in another company. It is very unlikely that you will be faced with such problems but, should it happen to you, you will know whom you consider to be in the right and what action that dictates. There can be no hard and fast rules, and you must trust your own conscience and judgment.

Your boss must know that you do not discuss business matters with your colleagues within the company or your friends outside it. (It is amazing how something told to someone with apparently no connection with the firm can get back and spread rapidly, often having been embellished on the way!) Never become involved with the power-seeking intrigues of company employees or with gossip of any kind.

There will be those who will seek to use you as a 'go-between' when they have criticisms and complaints about your boss or other directors (especially if you are secretary to the Chief Executive) because they think that you have influence in getting things changed. Indeed you may have, but you should avoid involving yourself in this way. Try suggesting to the critic that if he stops grumbling to you and tackles the person concerned directly, with some sound ideas for improvement, he will get more positive results. It is all too easy to find fault with the way things are organised; producing constructive plans for improving bad situations takes intelligent thought, hard work and time.

Initiative/imagination/ingenuity

From a practical point of view, these qualities mean that you are never beaten by what appears at first sight to be an insuperable problem. If you can clear your mind of preconceived notions of how it should be solved – but cannot be for some reason – and look at it from every angle, turn it inside-out and on its head, a solution will usually be found.

Tolerance/ability to relate to people at all levels

In any job, at any level, you will meet many people who do not 'see it your way'. Given the benefit of your interest and tolerance, you will find you can 'work it out' somehow. (See Chapter 4 Communication – Aiming for the best response.)

Willingness to learn

Be prepared to admit there is a lot you don't know! One of the great joys of living is that there is so much to learn that even if one had a thousand years at one's disposal one would never know it all. In the world of work, technology is advancing so fast – and the rate of change is accelerating – that we *must* open our minds and accept new ways of doing things that last year, or even yesterday, we thought we were experts in. Accept the chances you are offered to learn new skills.

Attention to detail

In a senior job, your boss will seldom bother to read through things he has dictated to you before he signs them, so you must be very careful that they are perfect in every respect. Read everything that comes in addressed to your boss, so that you are aware of the current situation. Make action lists, and each day make sure that items not accomplished are transferred to tomorrow's list. Ensure that your boss has all he needs in his office (and in his briefcase, if he wishes you to do this) – writing materials, papers for the next meeting, and so on. Keep him supplied with batteries for his calculator and refills for his ball-pens; keep the cocktail cabinet well stocked; tissues at the ready for his colds and aspirins for his headaches. Being a good secretary can be a combination of office manager, detective, hostess, nurse and mother!

Ability to work under pressure and cope with varying work loads

In a senior secretarial job this may be, at first, one of the most difficult things to adjust to. No two days will be the same. An ad hoc meeting can be called and a ten page report need to be typed for it in less than an hour; the 'phone may ring with repeated urgent messages – and you will have to stay cool, calm and typing fast! That same day you may also have to attend a meeting in the afternoon, reply to several urgent letters, confirm arrangements for an imminent business trip, chase the Accounts office for some vital figures, send flowers to your boss's mother for her birthday – and find time to get out and buy a dress for an important occasion! That is just one day, or maybe a series of similar days. It may be followed by a completely 'dead' patch where you can catch up, reorganise, recharge your batteries, go to the hairdresser – and sit and wait for the excitement to start all over again. During these flat periods, your boss may be intensely busy and so you will see next to nothing of him either – not even for signing of the outgoing mail because there will not be any! It takes a bit of getting used to, but the ability to remain fresh, interested and ready to attack the next panic situation calmly and effectively is something you acquire with practice.

Ability to adapt to changing situations

This can merely be a repetition of the above – after all, the job is bound to be full of 'changing situations'. It can also mean the ability to accept a new Chairman – perhaps even a new boss; the company may move its premises or be merged with or taken-over by another firm; jobs you used to do may be given to someone else or put onto the computer. Accept the change, whatever it may be, with an open mind and optimism. Find out just what it means to you and your job satisfaction before you make any comment or decision about it. If, after giving the new set-up a fair chance, you find it is perfectly ghastly – don't just continue to sit there gritting your teeth and feeling miserable – do something positive!

Willingness to accept the 'collaborator's role'

You are your boss's assistant, perhaps his 'right-arm', but not his deputy. His place in the hierarchy of the firm confers nothing of

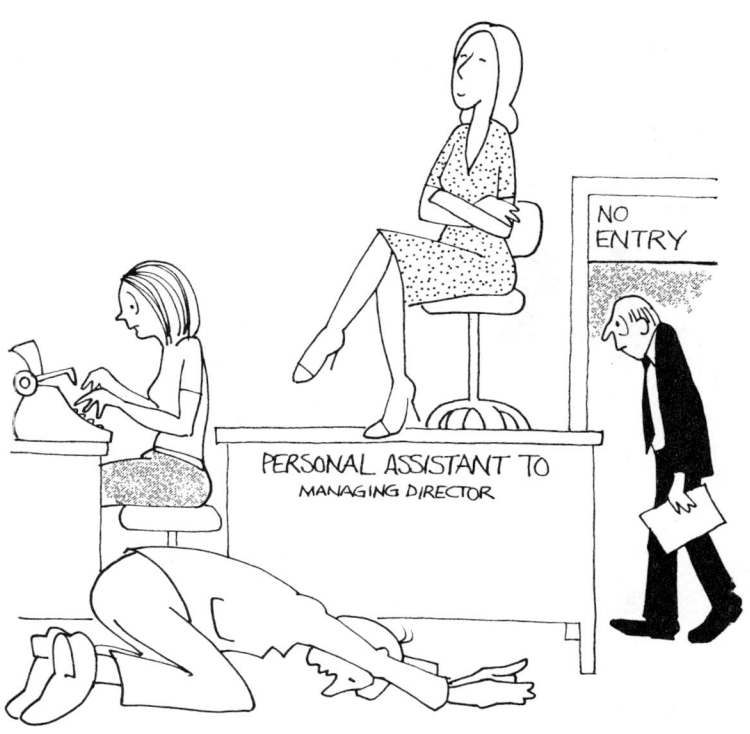

'His place in the hierarchy confers nothing of his status upon you.'

his status upon you. You are employed at your own level (possibly a senior one, but certainly not as senior as your boss and his fellow directors). So long as he is successful and seen to be so, your part in his success needs no commendation. Your attitude to other senior secretaries and middle managers will be from your rank in the organisation and not from your boss's. He may be the Chairman and major shareholder, and a law unto himself, but that is not your role nor is there any reflected glory in it. The senior secretary who considers herself 'above' members of management junior to her boss is not only deluding herself; she is anathema to her colleagues and a liability to her chief.

Resilience and a sense of humour

These two last mentioned qualities are by no means the least. The ability to accept setbacks and criticism with good grace is an attribute to be cultivated. If you can give your utmost effort to a task, have it go unnoticed, unused – or even totally rejected – and be able to shrug, smile and not let it upset you, you will enjoy

'The ability to accept setbacks and criticism ...'

your job much more and be a great deal easier to get along with. A sense of humour doesn't just mean laughing at the boss's jokes; seeing the funny side of difficult situations can redeem many a near disaster.

Summary

- Believe in yourself and develop your abilities
- Care for other people
- Make the best of your looks
- Be adaptable and ready to learn
- Maintain a sense of humour

3 Finding the job you want

Deciding where to work

In order to decide whether you prefer the atmosphere of a large company or a small firm, you will need to try both. It is important for someone setting out on a career as an executive secretary to obtain the widest possible experience in the early stages. Even if you feel from your self-knowledge that you will prefer one or the other, it will help you in your career to know how the other half lives, and how different types of business operate.

After qualifying in the basic skills and taking a junior position in one or two companies (possibly continuing your secretarial education by studying for a Secretarial Certificate or Diploma at evening classes), consider working for a secretarial agency as a 'temp' where you will get the opportunity of trying, for short periods and with no commitment to stay, a large number of different environments and duties. This will give you a good idea of the differences in style, methods of operating, opportunities for growth and so on between businesses. It is not suggested that you then fix your ideas once and for all on the sort of position you want for life, but by taking the time to find the right job in the right company where you can envisage staying for, say, three to five years, you will be adopting the 'career attitude' to working as a secretary and not regarding what you do as just a job or as a stepping stone to becoming an executive, film star or model. Of course, it may turn out that you do go on to some quite different career or 'change sides of the desk', but your aim in reading this book should be to become a first class executive secretary first!

To put the pros and cons of one type of business against another is something only you can do for yourself. In this section of the chapter I have tried to show some of the differences in the secretary's role in large and small concerns.

Each individual will know when they have found the 'right' atmosphere; whether the tasks to be undertaken appeal to them; whether the attitudes of colleagues and management are good from their personal point of view and whether a job is capable of growing as they themselves develop.

The large company – advantages

In the large company there will often be a good chance of promotion as job vacancies are almost always notified to staff before they are advertised to outside applicants. You will have a sound background knowledge of the company for which you work and your employers will know how capable you are. This will give you a considerable advantage when applying for the job you want when it becomes vacant.

A large company will probably have premises designed to add to its prestige and your office will usually be well equipped and well furnished. With such a company there is likely to be a forward-looking attitude to the use of modern machines and systems such as word processors, electronic typewriters, computers, fast and superior photocopiers, collators, etc. There will be fewer routine tasks for you to be personally responsible for, thus giving you a better opportunity and more time to provide real support for your boss in the planning and execution of his job.

There will be many centralised services for your use; postal, reception, reprography, filing, accounting and so on. More in-company expert advice will be available to you so that you will not feel you are on your own when dealing with problems. There will be others more qualified than you to take on specialised tasks that do not come directly into your sphere.

'There will be many centralised services for your use . . .'

There will often be the opportunity for you to specialise in your chosen field – finance, public relations, market research, law or personnel – and perhaps receive training at the company's expense. When you wish to move on you will have become an 'expert' in that field and be able to apply with confidence for a more senior job within that discipline in another company.

From the large numbers of staff employed you are more likely to find congenial social contacts and make friends. Many large companies have sports and social clubs, drama groups, debating societies, subsidised cafeterias, and offer additional benefits like interest-free loans, free private medical insurance and pension schemes.

The large company – disadvantages

There are some disadvantages which must be weighed against the advantages in a large company. For instance, there will be more staff on a similar level to yourself and therefore less chance to appear outstandingly good. In other words, the competition will be fierce and you will need to be aggressive in your approach if you are to achieve the promotion you want.

Although you will not have to carry out your own routine tasks when services are centralised, you will often find that the timescale for completing a job is longer than when you do it yourself. What you want done will have to wait its turn in a queue of what others want done. You may ask for a report to be photocopied and collated but, if the duplicating section is busy, it may be days before your finished reports are distributed.

Although there will be opportunities to specialise there will also be a tendency to become somewhat parochial. If you work in the Sales Department you may become a specialist in sales practices and procedures and feel that you do not need to know very much about how the rest of the company functions. You could become partisan in your views on what is really important to the business – namely, sales!

There will be an unwritten 'rule book' (in certain large concerns and in all government and public services, there is a written rule book) and you will have to abide by those rules. There will be 'correct' ways of doing things and you will find it more difficult to take decisions on your own initiative. Getting a decision from your boss on even relatively simple questions may need reference by him to his boss, then possibly to a committee or two, and weeks may pass before you get that decision and are able to take action. The decision may be to do exactly what your commonsense and experience told you was right in the first place, but according to the rules you would have been out of order to do anything without consultation 'through the correct channels'.

There may be a strict attitude to time-keeping, when you may take your lunch break, what you may wear, whether you may smoke and so on. These attitudes may not appeal to you, but if you work for a company where they apply, then you will have to conform in order to succeed.

The small firm – advantages and disadvantages

It is difficult to define the conditions in a small firm as being 'advantages' or 'disadvantages'; it all depends upon your viewpoint and the small firm concerned. The main advantage might be that you will feel part of the management team and have a real opportunity to influence the way the firm is run. On the other hand, you will probably have to help out in many menial tasks.

You may be working for more than one person or it may be that there is only one 'boss' who is himself responsible for all the different aspects of managing the business. Either way you will most definitely need to know a great deal about how the company functions, what its aims and plans are and how they are to be achieved.

'In a small firm you will be called upon to fulfil a more varied role.'

You will also be called upon to fulfil a more varied day to day role. You will have to be prepared to carry out most of the administrative tasks yourself. Instead of having a Telex operator (or section) you will need to operate the machine. In the absence of a Despatch Department, you will find yourself wrapping and posting parcels. Without a Transport Section, you will probably be the most likely person to chauffeur the boss or collect visitors from stations or airports. You may also be responsible for arranging to have the company's vehicles serviced, renewing road fund licences, MOT certificates and generally be in charge of arranging deliveries and collections.

You will probably be asked to undertake responsibility for a number of bookkeeping tasks, for ordering and arranging payment for goods, for liaising with customers, chasing them for payment and various other jobs that in a large company would be done by specialists.

You will certainly not have the chance to specialise, but you will gain an overall knowledge of the intricacies of running a complete enterprise and, when you decide to move on, you will be competent to undertake a job in any section of a larger business.

If you are virtually the only secretary/administrator there will be no chance of promotion to a more senior job in that field. However, as the business grows – and you can have a direct influence on that growth – you will effectively be promoted *within* the job, since you will recommend the right time to take on more staff and will be the one to select and train them. Although your job title (eg Personal Assistant to the Director) may stay the same, your responsibilities, authority and the actual work you undertake and organise will be growing and changing.

It cannot be said that small is more beautiful than big – or vice versa. It all depends on you and what will suit your personality, abilities and needs. In any company you choose to work for – large multinational or small 'family firm' – you should look for:

Opportunity – the chance to use your abilities, to improve your skills and to develop yourself in the job

Recognition – the knowledge that you will be considered as a person who has something worthwhile to contribute; be accepted as an individual and be treated fairly

Security – the assurance that the company is sound; the ability to plan ahead with the confidence that effort and enthusiasm will be rewarded by promotion and better pay and working conditions

In summary, when deciding where to work, remember to set out with an open mind, ready to learn and assess; take your decision on where to stay only after finding out how different companies function and making an assessment of what each environment has to offer you; look for opportunity, recognition and security.

Where to look and how to succeed

Before applying for a job you need to know:

a yourself and what you have to offer
b the job situation best suited to your needs and abilities
c how to set about finding it

Yourself and what you have to offer

Begin by making another self-appraisal but this time in relation to your work capabilities. Write a list of what you consider to be your strengths and weaknesses. For example; are you capable of dealing with varying work loads, keeping calm in a crisis, good at helping others with their problems, a self-starter? Have you the ability to write clearly and concisely, to set out a page of typescript that looks attractive?

'... are you capable of keeping calm in a crisis?'

On the debit side of the list be truthful. If you genuinely hate typing columns of figures (or balancing them), are fearful of making decisions or are easily upset by aggressive people, make a note of it. It does not mean that you are stuck with these attitudes, but simply that you must consider your ability to correct them. Initially, it would be sensible to rule out applying for a job where you will be called upon to do the very things that do not appeal to you. It is surprising, however, how many people think they are incapable of, say, bookkeeping, just because they have never been called upon to find out how and why it is done.

Any bad points that you list should be looked at objectively and you should consider ways of improving on or eliminating them. If you feel you lack the confidence to write well, make the effort to improve (Chapter 1 gives a few examples of how to do this). In writing letters always consider the recipient and what he or she will need to understand (see Chapter 4 Communication). Are you nervous of meeting people for the first time? Remember that this may also apply to the person you are meeting and that by adopting a relaxed and friendly attitude and considering their needs rather than your own, you are helping yourself to become more confident.

The job situation best suited to your needs and abilities

Many of the attributes and deficiencies you have discovered in your self-appraisal will give indications as to the sort of job you should look for initially. If it is clear that you are an extrovert, at your best when meeting new people and dealing with challenging situations, you will be looking for a job where you can be given a chance to use these qualities. You will probably be most satisfied in an extending and volatile environment and should look for a position in, say, publishing, public relations, advertising, sales or the communications media, where you will be able to use and develop your talents to the best advantage.

If, on the other hand, you can see that your capabilities lie in dealing with work of an administrative nature and you prefer to work quietly out of the limelight, you will be looking for a more structured situation where you 'know where you are' and can plan your days without too many last minute changes. A professional background – banking, finance, academic or legal office – will probably be more likely to offer this atmosphere. Obviously there are financial and legal concerns that are far from structured or calm, and situations in public relations and sales where, for all the client contact you have, you might as well be on a desert island, but make sure you discover this at your interviews!

Ask yourself where your major interests lie. Are you profit oriented and interested in 'the business' of business? Would you prefer to work in a service to the community? Are you attracted by the world of art and design? Do you care more for the people and the environment where you work than for the actual content of the job? Will being the personal assistant to the Chairman/ Managing Director, no matter what the business, be your prime objective?

You will already have assessed the opportunities available in large and small companies. Do you think you would be happier and work better in the more sophisticated environment of a very large company, glad of all the various services provided? Do you want a company where the chances of promotion within the same group are good? Or would you prefer an informal 'family' atmosphere where you know everyone, will be called on to do a variety of jobs and will get the opportunity to play an important part in the business? There may be little chance of promotion to another more senior post within the company but more prospect of developing the scope and responsibility of the job you have, since your efforts will be easier for management to observe and appreciate.

You will have had one or two permanent jobs and perhaps worked with a good secretarial agency investigating the market as a 'temp' and trying as wide a variety of companies and roles as possible. You will have decided what appeals most to you and the sort of background where you could work at your best.

How to set about finding it

Once you have decided what you want, there are a number of ways of finding out about jobs that are available:

- Reading the situations vacant columns in the Press
- Staff employment agencies
- Taking the initiative and writing direct to companies that appeal to you
- Learning of a job vacancy from someone you know
- Looking for promotion within the company you already work for via its Personnel Department

Situations vacant columns in the Press
When you read an advertisement for a vacancy that seems to meet your requirements, reply in precisely the form that the advertisement indicates. This may be:

a to send a letter giving details of your education and past career (sometimes referred to as a curriculum vitae or 'cv')
b to request that the advertiser sends you an application form for completion and return
c to telephone for an interview

The letter of application and cv Remember that the purpose of the letter is to get you an interview to discuss the job. Study the advertisement carefully to make sure that your reply gives the information the advertiser wants to read. Write a short covering letter stating where you read about the vacancy, why it appeals to you and what you feel you can offer. In your cv state where you are working at present, your reasons for wishing to leave, list your previous jobs and length of service (emphasising any facets which directly relate to the job you are applying for), your education and examinations passed.

Here is an example of a typical advertisement, and Figs 1 and 2 show a possible reply and cv.

SECRETARY required to act as personal assistant to the Public Relations Manager of a major international chemical company with offices in SW1. This is a responsible position calling for experience, initiative and enthusiasm. Please send handwritten reply together with typed cv to Box 678 quoting reference PRM.

Flat 266
269 Ashley Grove
LONDON SW3
16 September 198–

Ref PRM
The Advertiser
Box 678
The Morning Post
29 Bridge Street
LONDON SW9

Dear Sir

Your advertisement in today's edition of 'The Morning Post' for a secretary to the Public Relations Manager interested me immediately.

I have just over two years' experience in public relations and am keen to continue in that field as I find it exciting and challenging. I am seeking to change my job only because within the small company for which I work there is very little chance of promotion for many years.

I enclose brief details of my education and career as requested and look forward to hearing from you.

Yours faithfully
Jane Seymour

Fig 1 A letter of reply to an advertisement

```
Name:      Jane Seymour                    Age:       23

Address:   Flat 26b
           269 Ashley Grove
           LONDON SW3                      Telephone: 01 600 2345 (home)
```

Present position

Lyle Enterprises Ltd (Public Relations Consultants), London W1
Secretary to Senior Partner from 6 February 198-

Previous experience

Wedgewood & Gray Ltd (Estate Agents & Fine Art Dealers), London W1
Secretary to Fine Arts Director from 6 June 198- to 30 January 198-

Reason for leaving: to work in public relations

Messrs Brown & Wilson (Estate Agents), Barmouth, Essex
Secretary to Junior Partner from 2 September 197- to 29 May 198-

Reason for leaving: to work for larger company in London offering more
                     client contact

Education

Westfield Comprehensive School, Barmouth, Essex from 4 September 197-
to 21 July 197-

GCE 'O' Level passes in: English Language
                           History
                           Mathematics
                           General Science

St Anne's Secretarial College, Barmouth, Essex from 10 September 197- to
4 July 197-

Passes in: Pitman's Shorthand (120 wpm)
                           RSA III Typewriting
                           RSA II Secretarial Studies

Personal interests

Fine arts, reading, films, television, tennis, squash and table tennis.
Presently studying for London Chamber of Commerce & Industry's Secretary's
Diploma by attending evening classes.

Fig 2 A curriculum vitae

'Informal atmosphere.'

Some euphemisms you will find (and should beware of) in the situations vacant columns:

'informal atmosphere'	chaos
'sense of humour essential'	you get all the rotten jobs and are expected to keep smiling
'must be willing to work as part of a team'	prepared to take dictation from anyone and everyone in the department
'part-time'	full day's work to be done in short hours
'reasonably numerate'	able to keep the books to trial balance
'varied work'	jack of all trades and master of tea and coffee making
'would suit college leaver'	not prepared to offer reasonable pay and frightened of comparisons with other firms
'willing to accept responsibility'	always blamed when things go wrong

Finding the job you want

Of course, there are many times when these phrases mean just what they say, but be prepared for the occasion when the above definitions are nearer to the truth – try to find this out at your interviews!

Completing an application form Many medium-sized and large companies make use of a standardised application form, and each question must be answered clearly and succinctly. Read the form through carefully before you begin to write on it. It is worth copying out the questions from the form, writing your answers beside them, altering these if necessary and then completing the form. This gives you a copy of the questions and answers to keep and the form will have no alterations or 'second thoughts' on it. If, as in some cases of rather poor design, the form does not give you enough space to put in all the facts you consider relevant, continue on a plain sheet of writing paper and indicate this in the appropriate place on the form.

In giving your reasons for leaving any past employment, never criticise your colleagues, superiors or anything about the company's policy. If there was genuine criticism of your previous employers which caused you to leave, make sure to phrase this in the most acceptable words and without emotion. Be brief – you can explain the situation better at an interview. The most acceptable reasons for leaving are in order to obtain promotion, better pay and/or working conditions, or if you changed your address and the journey to work was then too long or expensive. Always tell the truth in completing such forms, and deal thoroughly with job situations that relate directly to the position for which you are applying, mentioning only briefly those that have no relevance. Always remember to ask the permission of anyone whose name you are intending to give as a referee.

Telephoning for an interview Ask to speak to the person mentioned in the advertisement and begin by saying why you are ringing them: 'I am telephoning in reply to your advertisement in today's "Morning Post" for a secretary to . . .' Be ready to answer a question or two on your abilities and experience, and have a few questions of your own to ask about the company and the job. Keep the questions you ask to a minimum; what you ask will depend on your personal requirements of a job. Listen carefully to the information given and make a written note of it. Be clear about the time of your interview, with whom, and ask for directions for finding the address. Sound enthusiastic and confident – remember, first impressions are important.

Staff/employment agencies
When you apply to a staff agency it may be for a specific job advertised in the Press or displayed in the window of the agency, or it may be that you decide on an agency and tell them your

abilities and requirements. In either case you should regard this encounter as your initial interview. You will want to impress the staff you see with your capabilities just as much as the person who will employ you (see The interview on page 39). You will be asked to fill in an application form or card (or a member of the agency staff will ask you questions and complete this for you) and what has been said above about application forms applies.

The staff of the agency may also want to test your shorthand and typewriting skills. The staff will also ask you about other experience you have, such as a knowledge of word processors, telephone switchboards, teleprinters, administration, bookkeeping and so on, in order to form a comprehensive picture of what you have to offer.

Be as precise as you can in describing the sort of job you are looking for and ask questions of the interviewer to find out all he knows about the job on offer. The best agencies make sure that their interviewers visit their clients to take instructions about vacancies and about the person ideally required to fill them. The agency will telephone the prospective employer to arrange an interview for you and will give them the facts about your past career. It is then up to you to present yourself really well and to find out all you want to know about the job at the interview.

All charges for the services of a staff/employment agency (as opposed to a firm of staff consultants or advisers) are paid by the company who engages the agency and not by the applicant.

Writing direct to companies that appeal to you
You are more likely to do this if you live somewhere where not so many jobs are available or advertised. It is fairly unlikely that you will find what you want immediately, but if you want to work for a specific company, are not particular about the department you start in and are in no great hurry to change jobs, it is well worth trying.

A letter along the lines of the one in Fig 3 on page 38 should get you an interview with the Personnel Department and your letter put on file for any future appropriate vacancy if none exists immediately. Telephone the company to find out the name of the Personnel Manager (or whoever is responsible for engaging staff) before you write your letter.

Learning of a job vacancy from someone you know
In this case it is probably best to telephone the Personnel Manager and explain how you learned of the vacancy, and ask if you may make an appointment to visit him to discuss the job and tell him about yourself. You may be asked some questions

```
                              (Your address and telephone number)

                                                              (Date)

    Mrs Felicity Kaye
    Personnel Manager
    ABC Manufacturing Company Ltd
    Mill Road
    LONDON   N1

    Dear Mrs Kaye

    I am writing to ask if there is likely to be a secretarial
    vacancy in your company in the near future. Most of all,
    I should like to work in public relations or publicity but
    would be prepared to start in any department with the hope
    of a transfer into this field whenever possible.

    I am 23 years old and unmarried. I have five years'
    secretarial experience and can provide good references.
    Enclosed is a brief history of my education and job
    experience. My reason for wanting to leave my present job
    as secretary to the Senior Partner in a firm of public
    relations consultants is that, after two very happy years,
    I can see no prospect of real challenge or job development
    beyond my present level.

    Perhaps there will be an opportunity to visit you to discuss
    in more detail what I think I can offer as an employee, and
    I look forward to hearing from you.

    Yours sincerely



    Jane Seymour
```

Fig 3 Letter written direct to a company

over the telephone (so, again, be prepared) or he may send you an application form to fill in and return by post or take with you to an interview.

Promotion within the company you work for
This is the most straightforward way to improve your position if the occasion arises. The company already knows about your background and abilities and you will only need to arrange to see the Personnel Manager to talk over the possibilities. Take as much care with this interview as with one for a job outside the company and present your case for promotion clearly and with enthusiasm. Remember, you are still 'applying' for a job!

Points to remember when applying for a job

1 The purpose of the application (letter, form or telephone call) is to get you an interview.

2   Draft your application first and rewrite it until you are satisfied, making sure that you write what the advertiser wants to read, and remembering to quote any reference number or code if indicated.
3   Emphasise the qualities and experience you have that relate to the position advertised. Mention only briefly those that do not.
4   Tell the truth, but keep in mind point 3 above.
5   Type (perfectly!) your letter unless specifically asked to write it in your own hand.
6   Make a copy of what you send for your own reference.
7   Use good quality writing paper of a sensible size and a sufficiently large envelope to ensure minimum folding.
8   Read through your letter and cv or application form very carefully *twice* before sending it to make sure there are no mistakes.

The interview

Before the interview
You have applied for the job and received an invitation to attend for interview. If this invitation is by letter, and even if not specifically requested to do so, you should confirm that you will attend. But *before the interview* there are a number of things to be done.

1   Find out as much as you can about the company and what it does. If it is a large company and you have time before your interview date, you can write to the company and ask for any literature they have available on their product or service. You can consult your public library for such reference books as *The Stock Exchange Official Year Book*, *Jane's Major Companies*, *Who owns Whom*, etc. If it is a local company, you may well know someone who works or has worked there and you can get their views.

2   What are you looking for in the company? As a career-oriented secretary it should include:

opportunity – a climate conducive to growth (its own and yours)
recognition – of the abilities of its employees
security   – good financial standing and a growing profit record

You will have your own thoughts on priorities, so make sure you are clear what they are.

3   What are you looking for in the job? Write yourself a list of questions to ask at interview. These will be personal to each applicant but can include anything from finding out about working hours, length of paid holidays, whether you will have an office of your own, to asking for a clear definition of what responsibility/authority/prospects the job offers.

4 What are you looking for in your immediate boss? Ideally, he should be:

fair and loyal to the company and its employees
competent and interested in doing his job well
concerned with meeting his deadlines
able to delegate and control
clear in his instructions to his subordinates
courageous in taking decisions and in making sure that decisions are taken
willing to keep you informed of all commitments that concern you

If he has a sense of humour, lack of prejudice, and flexibility of mind too, you really will have found the 'superboss' and you may not need to read Chapter 8 Advancement! However, most of us find only ordinary human beings to work for and part of our job is to minimise their shortcoming and maximise their abilities.

5 What have you to offer? Your self-appraisal should be consulted again before the interview. Plan constructively how to highlight your good points. Consider what experience you have had that is relevant to the job you are being interviewed for and make a note of this to mention at the meeting.

6 Find out exactly how to get to the interview address. If it entails a journey with which you are unfamiliar, it is worth buying a map or transport timetable, or even having a rehearsal before the date so that you know how long the journey takes.

At the interview
Having done all your preparatory work you are ready for the interview. Aim to arrive about ten minutes before the arranged time. Take with you any references you have, certificates of proficiency and a job description of your present position. You may not be asked for these, but take them anyway. The job description is very useful as it clearly defines your present responsibilities and will save the interviewer time in asking questions about what you do. If you do not have a very demanding job, at least you will have a starting point to discuss the things you feel capable of – possibly this lack of responsibility is one of your reasons for wanting to change jobs.

Take a shorthand notebook and your pen or pencils in case your prospective employer wishes to test basic skills. This does not happen often in applications for senior jobs as these abilities will be taken for granted, but should your prospective boss have suffered from a secretary who had poor basic skills he may be wary of taking anyone on trust, however bright they appear to be.

There are things to look for. Pay particular attention to the other people you see – the receptionist or commissionaire, the other workers and the secretary who is leaving. Try to assess the atmosphere of the place – do people appear confident, efficient and enthusiastic? How clean and tidy are the offices? What does the secretary's office look like? How tidy are your prospective boss's office and desk?

Look very carefully at your interviewer and listen attentively to everything he says. Remember that he will probably be (as you are) on his best behaviour. Try to think about what he does not say as well as what is said. Are you getting the impression of an open mind? Remember that it is essential for the boss/secretary relationship to be based on mutual respect and understanding.

Chapter 2 dealt fully with your appearance and attitude but it is worth remembering that you should wear at interview the sort of clothes and make-up you would wear normally to work, rather than 'dressing up' for the occasion. Indicate your willingness to take advantage of any suitable training courses available and, of course, if you are already attending any further education classes say so!

You will be feeling confident, at ease and receptive because the preparatory work you have done will be reflected in how you look and how you react. Your attitude throughout the interview will be attentive and interested. You may be fortunate in finding that your interviewer is good at interviewing – in that case all you need to do is to answer his questions carefully and ask your own when invited to do so. You know what you are looking for in a boss and you will recognise the qualities you are seeking. You have made notes of the questions you want to ask about the job and about the company. You know the qualities and skills you can bring to the job and will find suitable opportunities during the discussion when these can be emphasised.

One thought to keep in mind all the time is that making the decision to work for *this* person in *this* company is an important step in your career. Will working here give you the opportunities you want? Will you be able to bring to this job something special? Do you see yourself working with this person in harmony and actively assisting him to do a more efficient job? If you have any doubts, express them. Ask about anything of which you are uncertain. It will not do your career any good if you present a 'false face' at your interview and subsequently discover that you have accepted a job that is no more satisfying than the one you were in before.

Fortunately, for most senior secretarial positions you will have the opportunity of a second interview. If you are offered the job after the first interview, before accepting you might request a second visit to the office. To the right sort of boss this will be perfectly acceptable. After all, it costs a company a lot of money to engage a new member of staff. It is in their best interests to make sure – or as sure as it is possible to be – that the person engaged is suited to the job and will stay in it for a reasonable length of time.

There will almost certainly be facets of any job you are offered which will not be ideal but ask yourself whether you can learn to live with them, or whether you might be able to change them, given time. If you know you cannot do either, and on balance there appear to be too many of them, then reject the job, however good the pay or luxurious the office, and go on searching.

After a number of interviews for jobs which you decide you do not want or which are not offered to you, you may feel rather dispirited, but it is not worth taking something in desperation if you feel it is not really right for you. Look long enough and put enough effort into looking and you will find the right job. If you cannot continue in your present job, do temporary work until you find what you want.

Points to remember for the interview
1 Be prepared beforehand with some knowledge of the company.
2 Be punctual.
3 Take with you all the necessary documents and 'equipment'.
4 Know what you are looking for – in the company, the job and your boss.
5 Be confident of what you have to offer and talk about your abilities as they relate to the job.
6 Don't be afraid to ask questions.
7 Be appropriately dressed and happy with the way you look.
8 Be attentive and courteous – relax and smile.
9 Be yourself; your interviewer could be someone you will be working closely with for a long time!

Making a good start in a new job

You have successfully applied for, been offered and accepted a new job. This is an exhilarating feeling and a great opportunity because it gives you a completely fresh start and a new role. You are facing the challenge of making a success of another step in your career and, with a little help from this book, facing it feeling efficient and enthusiastic!

Meeting and remembering people and facts

First impressions in a new job are very important. When you join a company, everyone (with the exception of those you met at interview) is a total stranger. If it is a large firm it will take you weeks to match names and faces to the heads of departments and their secretaries, and may take months to know who is who throughout the rest of the company. Initially, concentrate on learning about those with whom you will be in frequent contact. If you are joining a small firm, the number of people you have to remember will be manageable, but your impact will be greater.

Keep your eyes open and look with interest at people you meet. Many people who are simply shy acquire a reputation for being 'superior' or 'cold' because they are too nervous to look carefully at others' faces, ways of dressing and mannerisms, but it is doing just this that helps you remember those you meet. Think how pleasing it is to you to be remembered by name by someone you have met only once and meet by chance again. It boosts the ego and makes you feel more kindly disposed towards them, and more likely to recall them with pleasure in the future.

When you enter your office building in the morning and meet another employee, don't just say 'Good morning', but add their name, look at them and smile – even if you don't feel disposed to do so! You are impressing your personality upon them and, by giving them their name and looking at them, you are helping yourself to remember that name and the face that it belongs to. It is important to build good relationships with the people you work with, not only for yourself but for the person for whom you work. By getting to know you and learning to like you, others will feel more at ease when contacting your boss through you. By being an open, receptive person you are improving communication between your boss and his colleagues and workforce. Improved communications can only improve the business.

As soon as possible after you join the company, ask your boss for a copy of the organisation chart or 'family tree'. This will tell you not only who is who but will indicate the various chains of command. Used in conjunction with your own 'portrait gallery' of departmental heads (see below), this will enable you to get an overall picture of the company set-up very quickly. An example of a simple organisation chart is given in Fig 4 on page 44.

If you have an overlap period with your predecessor, ask her help in compiling a 'who's who' in the firm. If you begin the job after she has left, try to establish in your first week a friendly relationship with one of the other secretaries who has the time and is willing to help you to do this. Make a list of names and titles and leave space beneath each to add details. Do not make your comments too personal and certainly never derogatory (unless you carry your list with you wherever you go!) eg:

Dr Charles Fairbairne: BSc (London): Technical Director: Room 3 ext 219
Secretary: Anne Wilson: Room 4 ext 220
Dr Fairbairne is responsible for Technical Division employing:
    8 project managers
    12 electronics engineers
    22 drawing office staff
Tall, very thin, reddish curly hair; slight Scottish accent.
Seems withdrawn and preoccupied. Prefers malt whisky.
Married (Elisabeth) with two daughters (Kim 8 and Sandra 6).
Secretary (Anne) always ready to help on any technical points; reminders for Dr F best passed through her if results wanted.

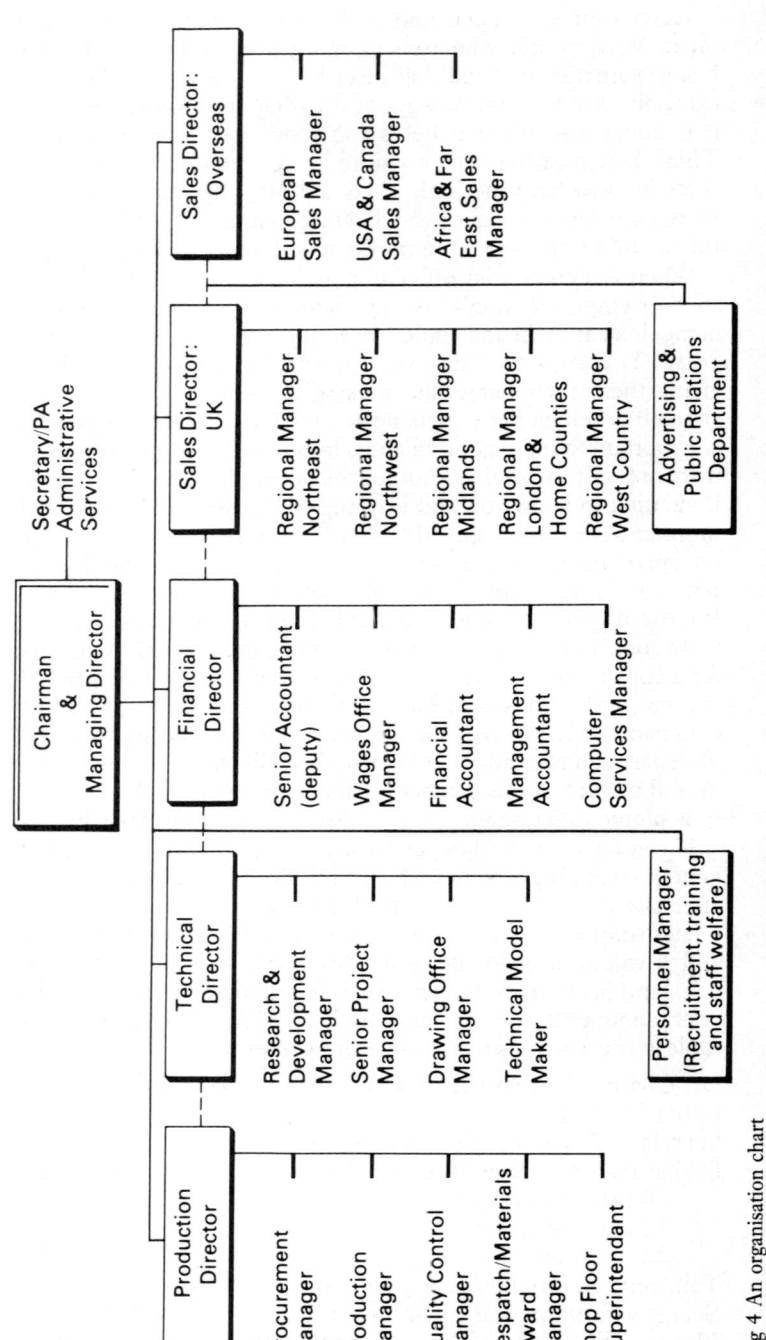

Fig 4 An organisation chart

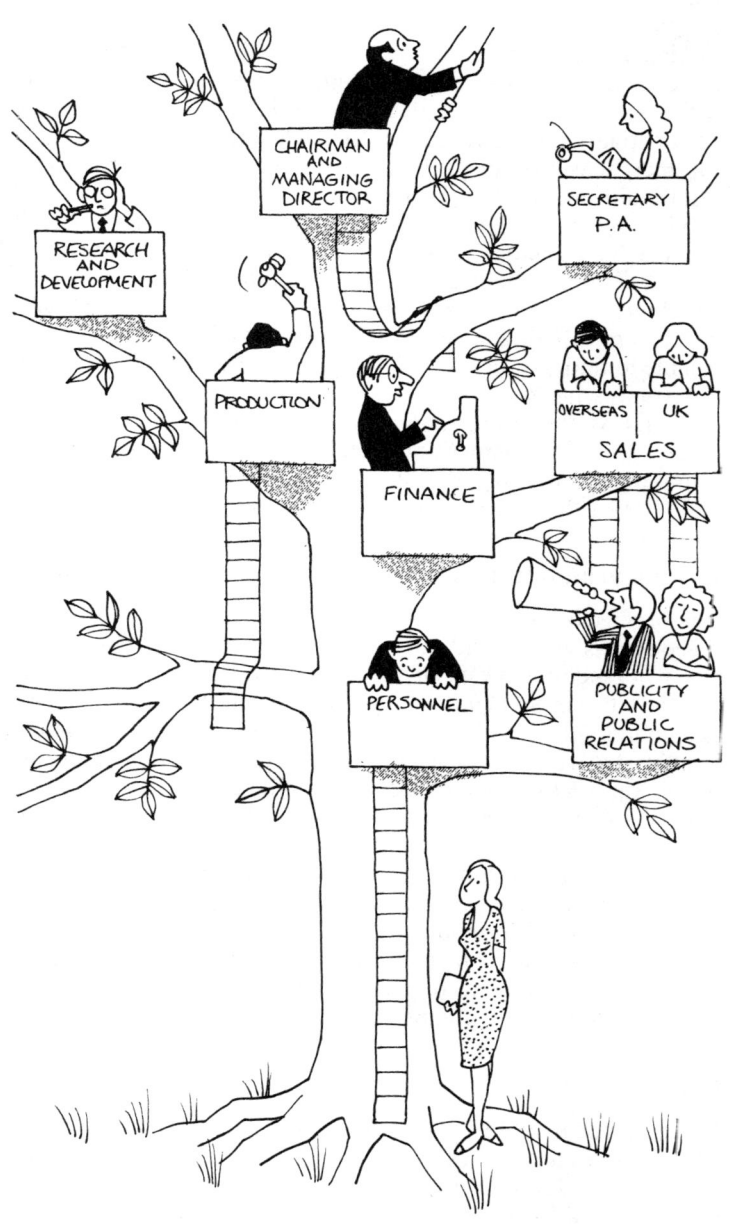

'... the organisation chart or family tree.'

You will not know all these details at once, of course, but can build them up as you go along. They will be useful for you to pass on to your boss should there be the need. Such things as making a note of his preference in drinks may seem trivial, but these small details can come in handy and often impress people with your thoughtfulness. If, for instance, your boss is likely to offer certain of his colleagues a drink when they are working late together, it will be helpful for him if you make sure the right drinks and mixes are in his cabinet.

The note about Mrs Fairbairne's first name would be useful for your boss to know so that he can remember to ask questions such as 'And Elisabeth is well, I hope?', and similarly for the two daughters. There are many other small details like this that are worth remembering, especially if your boss has not taken the trouble to find out for himself. By your efforts you will be able to improve his image.

So far as the rest of the Technical Division is concerned, make a list of the names and telephone extensions of the more senior people and rely on Anne to help you out with any queries and tell you the best person to speak to on particular subjects.

Getting to know the 'support team'

It is very useful in a new job to get to know the telephonists and receptionists and to find out more about their jobs. If you have never worked in that capacity you may consider it a glamorous or easy job. It may sometimes be glamorous but it is usually a very demanding job and, if not treated well, receptionists/telephonists have been known to take terrible revenge. Certain unpopular people can wait hours for calls and even be cut off in the middle of discussions – by accident, of course! A little influence can save you a great deal of time when you are really busy and will ensure that the telephonist will make calls for you or take messages with pleasure. Something done with pleasure is usually done properly and promptly.

Everyone in the company, from the Chairman to the porters and cleaners is entitled to your interest and courtesy. They are all part of the team that ensures the company's success.

Finding the time

You may well be thinking . . . 'when do I find the time for all this when I'm in there trying to learn a new job?' You will find that there are very few jobs that occupy you for every minute of every day and it will be possible to make the time for certain personal contacts. These 'extra' things are essential to doing a really good job. Look on them as an investment of time and trouble on your part to make you and your boss more productive. Apart from that, they make life happier and easier for everyone.

If you are genuinely shy of initiating relationships with others, what has been suggested may be difficult for you. Just take it slowly and remember that many of the others in your new company will be similarly shy. If, as the weeks pass, you can make the effort to get to know more people, you will learn a great deal about how the company functions and find it of benefit in doing a good job.

Adapting to new requirements

If this is your first advancement from secretary to executive secretary or personal assistant you need to understand the differences in responsibility. The role of the executive secretary/personal assistant can be defined as follows:

1 To provide an efficient 'clearing-house', both inwards and outwards, for the boss.
2 To save his time by being a receptive, intelligent listener and a priority-oriented action-taker.
3 To know how and when to follow up on instructions passed through her by her boss, so that he knows that immediately his instructions have had results he will be told of them. (He should never have to chase his assistant for the results of instructions given to her.)
4 To bring to his attention as soon as possible matters which require action on his part; and conversely not to bring to his attention at all (except 'for information only' items) matters which can be dealt with by others or by research on her part.
5 To screen his unscheduled visitors, as well as his mail and telephone callers, and judge whether or not a person really needs his attention or can be helped by another executive or herself.
6 To provide an efficient office service in such day to day routines as reading and answering correspondence, dealing with enquiries or problems by telephone or a visit, filing, attending to records and analyses etc, so that these matters never intrude in any way upon the time and energies of her boss.
7 To assist in creating an atmosphere of helpfulness and efficiency with her boss and all his associates and contacts, so that they will communicate through her with ease and therefore work more productively.

All these things may seem self-evident. But if you read carefully the last one you will see that it could mean some really hard work on your part. It comes down to you, the attitudes you adopt and your ability to compensate for any of your boss's shortcomings. If we look at two examples, both of people accepting jobs that involve working for someone with a similar temperament to their own, you will see that the need for the personal assistant to adapt is essential to harmonious and productive working – not just on a personal basis, but within the whole business. It is easy to work happily with a person you feel to be a kindred spirit, but one of your functions is to be a bridge between your boss and all those with whom he deals. It is you who must be prepared to make changes in yourself and in your work patterns. Never set out to try to change another's way of doing things; your actions will cause others' reactions, and the resultant chain of changes will benefit everyone *and* the company. So let us see how 'Angela' and 'Brenda' adapt to their new situations.

Angela is quiet and rather shy and has accepted a job as personal assistant to an equally quiet and shy Financial Director. Brenda has taken a job which she feels will suit her extrovert (and sometimes flamboyant) style, working for a successful, brash but charming entrepreneur who runs a property company. Angela discovers after a very short time that her boss is so introverted that he spends almost all his time at his desk, planning and computing, and avoiding all contact with his colleagues and the company's customers. His communications with others have suffered badly as a result, and everyone hesitates to contact him unless they have no alternative. This has cut him off from many areas where he and the company would benefit from his being involved.

Brenda adores the job she has taken – travelling with her boss, being wined and dined by his clients and so on – but becomes aware after a while that a number of them feel unhappy at their lack of information on progress and decisions taken. Her boss is rarely in his office for more than a few minutes at a time and, although he talks to a great many people, he rarely sends letters to anyone and seldom makes a written note of what is happening.

Both girls realise that there is a need for them to provide the 'compensating factor'. It would be easier for them to keep the status quo – after all, their own personalities are suited to it – but if they do this they will be only good secretaries, not good personal assistants. They will not be contributing to the success of the company as a whole. So Angela will take the necessary action to get to know and relate well with everyone her boss should know. She will tear herself away from her desk and planning and computations, and spend some time understanding other people's jobs and personalities. Brenda will politely refuse some of the invitations she gets to be out of her office and, instead, give the necessary time to record keeping, correspondence and follow-up. Angela will involve herself in more public relations work and less administration and Brenda will do the reverse.

'... compensate for any of your boss's shortcomings.'

'... compensate for any of your boss's shortcomings.'

Somewhere between these two simplistic extremes you, the personal assistant or executive secretary, and your boss are, whatever your temperaments, the two halves of a business whole. Since he is the boss, or 'senior partner', and you are the collaborator, you are the one who must make up for his shortcomings; not the other way round!

Summary

- First impressions are important – take special care to remember people
- In conjunction with the organisation chart, write personal 'portraits' of those who come within your immediate sphere
- Get to know people; convince them you care about them and their jobs and persuade them to care about you and yours
- Compensate for deficiencies in your boss in your approach to learning your new job

The chapters which follow make suggestions that you may find useful in working out a routine for the day, dealing with responsibilities of your own, writing minutes and planning itineraries. They do not set out to make rules for the way you must do anything. They are intended to start you thinking for yourself how to improve the way you approach your job. Each secretarial job is different from the next and only you, once you are established in a position, will know its particular needs and how best to adapt to them.

4 Communication

Aiming for the best response

Communication means making your needs, ideas and viewpoint known to and understood by others. How simple it sounds! It is simple, but it is not always simply done. The basic essential in communication is to put yourself in the place of the person to whom you are speaking or writing. Ask yourself what is their level of understanding, and what do you want to tell them? Examples of what you may want to convey range from the simplest request for the purchase and delivery of an item, to complicated instructions on how to accomplish a series of tasks, congratulation for or criticism of jobs done, recommendations for reorganising a system or systems, a report on what has happened in a particular area of the business, how it can be improved, and so on.

As an executive secretary you will be communicating almost all the time, liaising between your boss and other members of staff, welcoming visitors, delegating and motivating, using the telephone and telex, writing letters and memoranda, giving and receiving instructions.

On the telephone and face to face you need to be clear, to the point, brief and polite. On paper you need to be clear, to the point, not necessarily so brief – but twice as polite! If someone misunderstands you in a conversation they will be heard (or seen) to misunderstand and you can put it right immediately by rephrasing what has been wrongly understood. With a written document it is not so easy to clarify what puzzles the recipient. They will need to 'come back' to you, either verbally or in writing, and this may lead to further misunderstandings – and it certainly wastes time.

If you know the recipient you can assess his level of understanding and write accordingly. If you have never met him or dealt with him before, this assessment will not be possible. The position the recipient holds will not necessarily indicate his level of understanding; some very intelligent people do junior jobs – and vice versa! You must therefore be extra careful to organise your thoughts and express them simply and clearly.

Organising what you need to say

Always *think* about what you are going to say or write before you begin. Make a note of the essential points to be mentioned and those that you need to stress, such as a specific deadline or a particular effect that must be achieved. If you are talking to someone, *listen* very carefully to their responses. If you are face to face, watch their expressions, gestures and 'body language' to learn how they *feel* about what you are saying to them – whether they really understand your intentions and approve of them. To get the results you want from someone, they must understand what you want and in some cases why you want it. To get the very best results you need to have the recipient on your side and wanting to do what you require.

'... watch their "body language" to learn how they *feel* about what you are saying ...'

Your knowledge and use of English is one of your essential tools. You need to know how to construct a sentence, how to spell and punctuate and to have the ability to choose the right word or phrase to express exactly what you mean. You must care about how you express yourself. *How* you say what you have to say makes a tremendous difference to the response your communication receives.

Never assume that the other person will understand what *you* understand by listening to or reading the same words. In conversations there will be plenty of opportunity to ask questions and have them answered clearly. On paper you must make sure that the way you phrase a sentence leaves no room for misunderstanding. Get to the point early and fill in necessary background later. Set out the communication in such a way that essential information stands out from the main body of the typescript and important instructions or comments are immediately *seen* to be important. If you write in reply to something, deal with the points raised in the order they were presented. If it is an initiating letter, deal with the points in order of importance and/or timescale. If a reply to any point is necessary make this quite clear.

If what you have to say or ask is short and simple and no record is required, use the telephone. If you need a record of what is said, use the Telex. If your needs or replies are long and complicated and you can afford the delay of a few days, write a letter. If they are long, complicated and need decisions taken jointly, both write *and* arrange a meeting to discuss them fully.

If your boss is good at expressing himself you should adopt his style in letters he asks you to write on his behalf. If he is not, and perhaps does not care much about the good use of English, then try to compensate for this lack and write or rewrite his letters for him. Obviously there will be certain occasions when he will want you to write precisely what he has said, and even if you think you could express his sentiments better – don't!

Words are not always chosen carefully enough to achieve the best effect. If someone feels irritated or annoyed by a situation (not necessarily the one he is speaking or writing about) it is all too easy for that irritation to be apparent in his choice of words. In a conversation this can be overcome by the right riposte; we can be 'pulled up' by the appropriate phrase which makes us realise we are putting things badly or getting unnecessarily annoyed. When we let our annoyance have expression in the written word, however, the result is far worse since, by the time the letter is received, we will probably have the situation in much better perspective and have ceased to be annoyed by it. Our rude or thoughtless letter will be making the recipient cross and a chain of irritation will have been started.

Writing letters

Figs 5 and 6 on page 54 show two letters which convey the same facts but in different ways. The background is as follows.

The recipient is the Sales Director; the writer is the Managing Director of the same company. They are friends of long standing. The matters concerned were discussed over lunch the previous day and are confidential. Since the Sales Director is often away the letter is directed to his home address and not sent as a memorandum to his office.

Dear Charles

Since we had lunch together yesterday, I have been reconsidering the items we discussed and want to make clear my feelings on the following points:

1. Regular meetings: I still think these would be a waste of time, but as I said, I will go along with the idea if you really feel it is essential - if only for a few weeks.

2. Budget control: I agree that if we need to keep altering the figures because of our ineptitude in assessing needs in advance, then we ought to dispense with the yearly budget and produce figures more often - a monthly budget is more appealing - the whole system of forecasting needs looking at, and we should do that soon.

3. Visits of sales executives to the factories: As I said - probably a waste of time but as they have frequently requested to see 'new production methods' we might as well agree and have a trial run. I expect it to die a natural death pretty quickly.

Many thanks for the lunch.

Yours sincerely

Fig 5 Original letter

Dear Charles

Thank you for yesterday's excellent lunch. It was as usual a pleasure to be entertained by you, although on this occasion we were not in total accord!

I should like to clarify my feelings on the following points:

1. Regular meetings: As I said, I am not convinced of the necessity for a fixed weekly meeting but, upon reflection, I see no reason why we should not arrange to have them for a few weeks and review their worth after we have had a chance to see how they go.

2. Budget control: The yearly budget does seem to be becoming something of an anachronism and you are right in suggesting that we would do better to produce a monthly forecast. I feel that perhaps we should look at our whole approach to budgeting in the near future and will arrange a meeting shortly to initiate some thoughts on the subject.

3. Visits by sales executives to the factories: I am pleased that there should be an interest expressed by your people in seeing the works and in keeping in touch with new production methods etc, and will put arrangements in hand right away. So long as they are interested in coming, we shall be pleased to welcome them.

With kind regards,

Yours sincerely

Fig 6 Rewritten letter

The letter dictated has been drastically rephrased, but it still conveys the same message. The Managing Director actually agreed to do what the Sales Director asked, but he did it with poor grace. By eliminating the disgruntled and possibly offensive comments, the secretary has presented her boss in a better light. He may have been in a disagreeable mood when he dictated the letter, but there is no need to record the fact in print if you can convey precisely the same points politely.

Changing a letter like this does call for a real knowledge of the people concerned (both the writer and recipient) and, of course, the permission of the writer to do so. It needs a facility with language and a feeling for the smoother way of expressing things. If the boss's letter had been negative to all Charles's suggestions the task would have been a great deal more difficult, because rewording negatives to sound acceptable is not easy. It can be done, though, by giving sensible reasons for refusal, offering suggestions of alternatives and some hope of better things to come – if only in other directions.

It is a useful exercise in those inevitable slack periods at work, when you have done all the jobs you have put off 'until you can find the time', to think of pleasant ways of saying or writing unpleasant things. Imagine yourself as the recipient, or think how a friend or relative who is sensitive, would react to a tactless and unthinking letter. Remember, you are always seeking good results, and everyone reacts better to a well phrased, pleasant letter than a rude or wholly critical one.

It is not suggested that everything you or your boss writes should be sweetness and light. Obviously there will be occasions when it will be necessary for him to launch rockets at subordinates, criticise his peers or complain of inefficiencies in outside concerns, and these communications will need to be strongly worded. However, for the most part, the less aggressive and bad tempered one sounds the better.

Ideally, if you or your boss have something really unpleasant to impart, it is far better to make the opportunity to do it face to face. This gives the other person a chance to explain the reasons behind the action that is being criticised and to defend himself. Remember that if you commit yourself to the written word – and the accompanying delay in its receipt – you put yourself in a more difficult position to *improve* your phrasing or retract anything you then feel less strongly about. The really unpleasant things (such as a dismissal or end of a contract) should ideally be communicated face to face. In circumstances where this is absolutely out of the question, whatever is written must be very clear as to intent and, while it is right to mention any good points in the situation so that the recipient is not totally cast down, it must leave no loopholes for misunderstanding or argument.

The following letters demonstrate *a* how *not* to write when ending a contract (Fig 7), *b* a likely reply (Fig 8), and *c* how to accomplish the ending cleanly and politely (Fig 9). The background is as follows:

The company's advertising agency has made a number of mistakes over the past two years and is not now giving an efficient service. The agency is not responding quickly to requests for action, the charges are high and not always clearly justified; in short, it has gradually deteriorated from what, in the

---

Southern Delicatessen Meats Ltd
9 Brede Road
WINNINGTON
Berks

2 July 198-

Mr John J James
Welham & Langley Ltd
Advertising Consultants
Brandon Court
LONDON WC2 1ZZ

Dear John

Your agency has handled our account for over ten years, and during this period we have in general been well satisfied with your service. We remember with special gratitude the speedy and effective help you gave us in securing the business with the chain stores. After twenty years of developing the more traditional outlets our success in this sector of the market convinced us that this was the direction we should be taking and Bill Watson gave us a flying start in our efforts to improve our company image. Labels and letterheads incorporating the new logo are now coming into use and have been much admired.

We are now well into our twenty-fifth year and for some months we have been reorganising our sales force in line with rapidly changing market needs. A reappraisal of our advertising activities confirms the trend towards below the line activities which you yourself noted last year, and in 198-/8- promotional outlay will be higher than ever before.

Our expenditure on media advertising will therefore be relatively modest and, although I have absolutely no doubt that you and your staff would continue to give us your usual high standard of service, I fear that our account may well become uneconomic from your agency's point of view.

We have therefore decided to transfer our advertising business from the end of our planned year with you, ie 1 September, to another agency. Graham Ford & Associates have been handling our public relations for some years, as you know, and they have an exceptional knowledge and understanding of our requirements.

Yours sincerely

Jim

James Mitchell
Sales & Marketing Director

Fig 7 Letter 1

early days, was an excellent service. Another firm has done some similiar work for the company very well and is keen to acquire a good account. The Marketing Director has decided to terminate the agency's contract and pass the work to this other firm.

Welham & Langley Ltd
ADVERTISING CONSULTANTS

Brandon Court
London WC2 1ZZ

---

5 July 198-

Mr James Mitchell
Sales & Marketing Director
Southern Delicatessen Meats Ltd
9 Brede Road
WINNINGTON
Berks

Dear Jim

I was very surprised to receive your letter of 2 July and am completely at a loss to understand why you feel it necessary to make a change in your advertising arrangements.

I had thought that we had developed a good working relationship over the years and, as you recognise in your letter, we have given you a pretty good service.

Be assured that we would definitely not consider your business to be uneconomic and are very keen to continue to look after your account. Why don't we meet for lunch this week to discuss the matter further?

With kind regards,

Yours sincerely

J J James
Managing Director

Fig 8 The reply

The first letter is so courteous that its purpose is almost totally obscured. Of course the recipient is going to come back and fight for his life – he feels he must have a good chance of survival! The rephrased letter (see page 58) demonstrates how to write in a way that cannot be misunderstood or refuted, but is nonetheless polite. There is very little, if anything, the agency can say in reply to a letter like this, except to accept the termination gracefully and wish the company well with its new agency. It is quite clear that the contract will be terminated and why. The agency will be aware that they have fallen short in various areas and will realise that there is nothing they can now do to put things right. All in all (and because it was impossible to meet face

Southern Delicatessen Meats Ltd

9 Brede Road
WINNINGTON
Berks

2 July 198-

Mr John J James
Welham & Langley Ltd
Advertising Consultants
Brandon Court
LONDON WC2 1ZZ

Dear John

We have been clients of your agency for some ten years now, and at first the service we received was excellent. However it has not been so recently and, for a number of reasons, I am convinced that the time has come for us to part company:

1. During the past two years we have increasingly had to remind the agency of its commitments to our account, to ask for information we should have received - and would have received as a matter of course in the early years.

2. I personally have had to query certain charges and methods of billing.

3. We feel we need the sort of service that a young and hungry agency can supply - as you yourselves did when you were in that state.

We have found just the sort of agency we need in Graham Ford & Associates who, as you know, have been handling our public relations business for some time and doing a superb job.
We will transfer our account for advertising to them at the end of our planned year with you, ie on 1 September this year.

I want to thank you and all your staff for the help you gave us in our early years and which contributed so much to getting us off to a good start. We are particularly grateful to Bill Watson for his ideas and hard work in improving our company image and to all of you for your speedy and effective help in securing the business with the chain stores.

With every good wish for your continued success,

Yours sincerely

Jim

James Mitchell
Sales & Marketing Director

Fig 9 How letter 1 might have been written

to face for some reason) this letter has cut the link with little pain to either side. It has been done frankly, kindly and above all, irrevocably.

Dealing with less pleasant people

In your face to face communications you will sometimes have to deal with unpleasant people. If what they say is unkind or even downright rude it will be difficult to remain polite, but if you can manage to do so, it is more than likely that some solution can be reached. While you may never become friends with the person concerned, you may manage to find sufficient common ground to deal amicably with each other on future occasions.

There will be times when you have to be very positive in your refusal of someone's demands. An aggressive salesman or representative, for example, who has no appointment but who insists, in a bullying way, that he has an absolute right to see your boss can cause difficulties for you. Remember he has, after all, to do his job forcefully in order to succeed, but once he realises that you cannot be bullied into doing what he wants he will accept it. While you must learn to be absolutely firm in your denial of his 'right' to see your boss without an appointment, you can do it in such a way that the salesman will feel he has not lost face. He will know that he has in you someone who will at the appropriate time pass on his information so that he will still have a chance of making a sale.

Try always to establish good relationships with your colleagues and contacts, whatever their personality, and sustain these relationships by being helpful, fair in your judgments and consistent in your attitudes. If you are so pressed by urgent work that you really cannot spare the time to listen to someone, always make sure you get back to them as quickly as your work allows. If you promise to return someone's call or visit, be sure you do so, even if you feel that what they are going to say will be of little interest. Never let anyone waste your time; deal with what they have to say quickly and bring the conversation to a close tactfully.

When it is necessary for you to disagree with someone's point of view or to criticise something that has been done for you, do

'When it is necessary for you to criticise, do so in a quiet and ordered way . . .'

so in a quiet and ordered way, thinking of both sides of the argument. Make sure you know all the facts of a situation before you criticise. Be fair and listen carefully to the replies. Be constructive rather than destructive in your criticism; never let someone feel they have failed hopelessly (see Chapter 5 Responsibilities of your own).

Summary

- Know what you need to say and make a rough note of it before you begin
- Assess the recipient's level of understanding
- Get to the point quickly
- Give the necessary background information
- If replying, deal with items in the order they were presented
- If initiating, deal with items in order of importance or timescale
- Make clear any action that is necessary on the part of the recipient
- If speaking, listen/watch carefully for reactions
- Be prepared to rephrase and approach from another angle if not understood
- Involve the other party – make your proposals/instructions attractive; indicate how they might be achieved
- Always be polite, even if what you have to say is a criticism
- When rephrasing a letter written by someone else make sure you have the permission of the writer to do so; cover all the points mentioned in the original; alter only the tone and not the intent of the letter

5 Responsibilities of your own

As an executive secretary, you will be required to accept responsibility for the work you do and will not expect to be told how to organise your time. The first 'responsibility' you have, therefore, is to make the best use of your own talents and to plan the sensible use of your time.

Another and very important responsibility you have is to help your boss to make the best use of his talents and to do for him the tasks that are within your capabilities so as to lighten his load and allow him to use his time to good effect.

A third responsibility is concerned with using resources available to you, researching information yourself and delegating certain jobs. You may be in a position where one or more junior typists or clerks report to you and you will be required to set work for them, train them in routines new to them, check their work and, above all, motivate and enthuse them.

Planning your day

There will be a routine to follow for the day, around and in between which you will have the freedom to organise your other work. Such a routine would, as a rule, require you to be in your office before your boss is in his. This will give you a chance to check the diary again (you will have done this late the previous day, preferably with your boss), put together any papers your boss needs for his morning's meetings and work – gathering these from your 'bring-forward' or 'pending' file as appropriate – and open and read the post. If incoming letters are in reply to his, attach the copy of his letter and any ancillary papers to the reply so that he has the whole picture. Make sure also that he has sharpened pencils, pens, a clean blotter (if he uses one), a supply of paper for notes and a tidy desk to start the day with.

Assume that the diary looks like this for today:

0930	Regular weekly meeting with Sales Director
1030	To be joined by the four Sales Managers – new plans
1145	Interview (second) with shortlisted candidate for position of Chief Accountant – Mr James Fellows
1300	Lunch at Café Romano with Mrs Sheila Brown (the afternoon has been left free)
1930	Dinner at Guildhall. Vote of thanks to guest speaker

Your boss usually arrives at 0930 (and you get in by 0900), so yesterday you mentioned that his meetings started at 0930 and perhaps he would like to be in around 0920 to glance at any urgent post, messages or 'bring-forward' items which cannot wait.

Yesterday, when you looked at today's schedule, you made sure that your boss had more or less completed his speech for the Guildhall and looked through the application form and comments from the Financial Director about the applicant for the Chief Accountant's job.

You will have put together yesterday the files needed for today's meetings and will check that they are in the correct order this morning. The regular meeting with the Sales Director has a constant 'running' file which you keep in your cabinet and into which you put all relevant papers and notes of items which either party wishes to discuss.

This meeting is being followed by a joint meeting with the Sales Managers who will have come in from the regions specially. It is rare for the Managing Director to see them and today it is because of a proposed new venture. The Sales Managers do not know the details. You made sure yesterday that there are sufficient copies of the proposals to hand out at the meeting. Organise coffee for 1030 at the time when the Sales Managers join the meeting and there is a natural break.

At the end of the meeting with the Sales Managers, you will have the folder containing all Mr Fellows' details ready to take in. (The MD read through this yesterday and so does not need any time between meetings.) Mr Fellows may arrive a little early (like all keen applicants) and so you will have to entertain him and offer him coffee until your boss is free to see him.

It will take your boss 25 minutes to get from the office to the restaurant where he is giving lunch to Mrs Sheila Brown. As he is the host it would be preferable for him to arrive on time and so you must try to get him to bring the interview to a close by 1230 at the latest.

Your routine for the day has already been slightly changed in that you did not get time to go through the post in your usual way, but had to skip quickly through to see if there was anything really urgent that you could not deal with yourself. On a normal day (if there is such a thing!), your routine would be something like the following.

Post

Open and sort the post. There will probably be three or four main categories of incoming post:

a urgent – and for your boss's action
b interesting but capable of being dealt with at leisure

c of no direct interest to him and intended for another executive or yourself

d circulars and advertising material which you can put aside and look at later, pass on, file for future reference or throw away immediately

Take in to your boss the urgent and interesting items (*a* and *b*), attaching to them any previous correspondence on the subject plus any extra information if you have it. Write this extra information as a note, rather than telling your boss of it verbally when you go in; it will then be a permanent reminder and not something that he could easily forget. Include any 'brought forward' items that require his attention.

If it is going to be a busy morning it is quite likely that your boss will only look through the mail and not give any instructions on it. If this is so, take it away with you and re-present it in the afternoon. There are two basic reasons for this suggestion:

1 If you leave it with him you may not see it again for some time!

2 While he is occupied with other work or meetings, you can have another look at it and see if you can deal with it yourself. You will then only need to give him the reply letters to read and sign. He may not approve of what you have written and will then dictate his reply. This is not a waste of your time, however, because it demonstrates that you are keen to be of use in saving his (more expensive) time, and what you say may remind him of, or suggest to him, something he ought to be saying.

Pending or 'bring-forward' files

(See Chapter 1 – Filing and record-keeping for a full account.) Refer to your pending system each morning and evening just as you do with your diary. The evening check is to make sure that whatever is to be brought forward is in order and complete – and if not, to correct the situation. The following morning you will be taking action as indicated. Frequent and regular reference to the diary and/or bring-forward file is *vital*.

The afternoon routine consists of getting the outgoing post signed in good time to catch the last collection (marking up the file copies with any action needed and noting this in the 'bring-forward' system) and going through the next day's appointments with your boss. The last mentioned ensures that you both know where and when things are happening and that you can update each other on any meetings that have been suggested or fixed in the other's absence. If your boss is away from the office on a particular day, then of course you can only look through the next day's itinerary and prepare for anything that is indicated. If he is away a great deal of the time, persuade him to keep you in the picture about appointments he has made, when he telephones instructions or sends you tapes by post.

He may carry a pocket diary wherever he goes and have a desk diary in his office. Together with your own diary, this means you have to keep up to date on three lists of appointments and reminders. If your boss is really too busy to talk to you about what he has arranged to do, then ask him to lend you his pocket diary for a few minutes each day he is in the office.

It is essential that your diary is up to date and corresponds exactly with your boss's diary/diaries so that you do not arrange meetings that clash or allow insufficient time between appointments. Remember to let Reception know the names and expected times of arrival of visitors first thing each morning.

Routine jobs (other than regular filing) will be dictated by whatever position you hold. You may have figures to collate or compute, graphs to plot or other records to update, and you should always see that you do these routine jobs regularly because any record that is not current is worth very little.

Lightening your boss's workload

It has been suggested that you can do this by your handling of the post and the 'bring-forward' items. You can also do so by 'researching' for him. This simply means finding information that he needs. It can mean anything from looking up addresses and telephone numbers to getting information on what is happening in a field of activity that he needs to know about.

While you should never be afraid to ask your boss about something you do not understand, ask yourself first if there is another way to find the answer. Obviously, if you know he is not busy and it will take him only a few minutes to give you the answer that could take you hours to discover, then ask him. However, there will be times when you cannot ask him and then you will need to know how to set about finding out for yourself. Other executives and secretaries in your company will be in a position to help you with some queries, but you should know where to find the appropriate help outside the company.

Here are a few basic sources of information you will find useful to keep in your own office:

- Dictionary and thesaurus
- Address and telephone number file: a card index or a loose leaf book for the names of people you frequently deal with, complete with any additional useful information about them
- List of internal telephone extensions plus home numbers of executives closely associated with your boss
- A note of your company's (and your boss's, if different) bankers, insurance brokers, accountants, solicitors, etc
- Telephone directories, Yellow Pages, Telex directories

'Lightening your boss's workload.'

- Any specialist handbooks and trade and professional association directories relating to your company's/boss's interests
- British Rail timetables for journeys your boss makes frequently
- AA or RAC Members' Handbook
- A to Z street plans of London and other major cities
- Hotel and restaurant guides plus your own index of your boss's favourite places
- A simple encyclopaedia such as *Pears Cyclopaedia* is useful for information on historical, geographical, economic, musical, sporting events and background
- *The Post Office Guide*, if not already kept by your reception/postal staff, gives useful and detailed information on the services provided
- *The Office Companion*, published by Case Law Ltd (Cobham, Surrey), which includes a quarterly updating of very comprehensive information on everything from accomodation to entertainment, equipment, forms of address, services, transport and travel

Responsibilities of your own

Some other useful sources of information outside your office are:

- Public libraries: the librarian is a very helpful person. Most libraries keep copies of well known reference books such as *Who's Who, Burke's Peerage, Directory of Directors, Whitaker's Almanac, The Statesman's Yearbook, Willings Press Guide, Croner's Reference Books*, and so on. The librarian will also be able to tell you where to look if you ask for help.
- Professional or trade associations with which your boss is connected: the secretary or librarian employed by these associations will help you if your query comes within their scope.
- Government departments, county councils, embassies or high commissions, trade departments or legations, tourist offices: these are helpful resources for finding out what happens in their fields. Contact the appropriate embassy or delegation with any queries you have when your boss is intending to travel to the country they represent. Remember to use your Telex if you have long or complicated queries.
- The Financial Times Library and the Daily Telegraph Information Service: failing your local librarian, these two services will, when contacted by telephone, either give you the answer to your query or tell you where you can find the answer.
- The British Lending Library in Boston Spa, Yorkshire: if you are outside London and cannot visit the British Library personally to research anything out of the ordinary, the library in Boston Spa will find and send to you almost any book on any subject for a very reasonable subscription.

'Social' secretarial aspects

Your area of responsibility here may mean only sending Christmas, birthday and anniversary cards to your boss's friends and acquaintances (make sure you keep an up to date list of names, addresses and dates), or it may extend to choosing, buying and wrapping presents as well. However, it can involve anything from keeping a well-stocked cocktail cabinet and learning to serve drinks in professional bar style, to obtaining theatre tickets at short notice for a 'sell-out' show, or entertaining the families of business contacts from out of town while their husbands are in conference with your boss. You may also be asked to arrange buffet lunches at meetings or to set up and be the 'hostess' at business conferences or dinner parties.

You will need to know the best suppliers of food, drinks, flowers, etc and establish good relationships with them so that you can rely on them to provide just what is wanted, when and where it is needed. You will also have to develop a reasonable knowledge of food and drinks – wines in particular if you are to be in charge of selecting them. It is sensible too to know your own area and what it has to offer the visitor so that if called on to entertain someone you will be able to do this with confidence.

If this has been part of the preceding secretary's job, as you take over she will of course give you guidance on what is available and you will get off to a good start. If it is to be a new part of the job you will be dependent on your own personal knowledge and experience. Perhaps you are already blessed with a background and social life that has educated your palate and taught you the appropriate venues for various types of occasion, and so you will have few problems. If your lifestyle is different from the one in which you will be arranging social gatherings, then at first you will have to consult closely with your boss to find out not only precisely what he wants you to do, but how to do it. It is obviously difficult for someone who does not drink alcohol to choose the right wines, and equally difficult for someone who generally regards 'eating out' as a hamburger and chips to choose the menu for a five-course dinner in the town's best restaurant – or even to know which is the best restaurant! Don't despair; it is always possible to acquire this knowledge.

'... someone who generally regards "eating out" as a hamburger and chips can have difficulty.'

Responsibilities of your own

It is not sensible here to include lists of food, wines, cocktail mixes, quantities to be purchased or recommended restaurants. Telephone directories (Yellow Pages) for your local area will tell you who and where your suppliers are. It is up to you to contact and visit them to gain their support in helping you to provide the necessary service to your company.

It would be surprising to hear of any establishment (hotel, restaurant or conference centre) where, if you contact a member of the management and explain your position (ie that you are a novice at organising a function) you will not meet with sympathy and an enthusiasm for proving to you – and of course to your company – that they have everything you need. On the whole, experts enjoy teaching the uninitiated and, once again, it is far better to admit to your lack of knowledge and demonstrate an eagerness to learn than to pretend you know it all already.

Your local library will have many books on the subject of food and wine, flower arranging, etiquette and even how to set up business conferences, so start by reading some of them to gain a background. Many secretarial handbooks also give advice on types and quantities of food suitable for business lunches or dinners and so on. Your boss, and probably other executives in your firm, will be more than happy to help you on these subjects. If it is important enough for your services to be used in this way, it will be important enough for your company to spend some time, thought and money on making sure you learn how to be of maximum help. Encourage your boss to be helpful to you by your enthusiasm for learning, by research on your own and by suggesting ways in which the company can help you.

Report writing

At some stage in your career as an executive secretary you will probably be required to write a report. You may be asked to give advice or you may take the initiative yourself in deciding that a situation needs reform. Whatever the subject you are to write about, you must first ask and obtain the answers to these essential questions:

a What purpose is the report to fulfil?
b Who is to receive it?
c When must the report be completed?

The answer to *a* will enable you to gather the right information and put the facts together in the most appropriate sequence and style to achieve its aim. The answer to *b* will allow you to assess the level of understanding of the recipient. The answer to *c* may indicate that, if your timescale is short, you will not be able to research as thoroughly as you would like. You will then need to make it clear that the report takes the 'broad view' and may contain a certain amount of opinion or unchecked fact. If the time available is longer, then more background information can be sought and checked, gathered and analysed, and displayed in the best possible way, perhaps with charts, statistical tables, etc. In either case, there are four stages in preparing a report.

1 Establish purpose and form Before you set off to gather your input information, draft a series of headings and subheadings of the topics you feel should be covered – your 'contents page'. If someone else has asked you to write the report consult them again to see if they wish to add anything to your 'contents' or leave anything out. This second consultation also enables you to make quite sure that your understanding of *a*, *b* and *c* above is correct.

2 Research and collation There will be a number of areas in your 'contents' headings that can have answers provided by others. For example, if you need to know how cumulative sales figures for the last five years compare with those for the five years before that, the sales administration office will let you know these basic figures without you having physically to search the files for them. If you are asking for something specific and precise – say, only the June figures for one product over only the past three years – be exact in saying that this is *all* you want. It is very irritating for someone to spend hours searching through old files, compiling lists of figures of which only a few are going to be used.

From your contents list it will be evident what information you need to collate (from your own and from others' research). Once you have gathered your information you need to consider carefully how to use it to achieve your aims.

3 Drafting There is no set pattern for report writing, but a general rule for ease of reading would be to:

a decide on its title
b write a brief introduction explaining the reasons for the report, its purpose and the conclusions reached
c list the headings and subheadings of the report's contents
d present the argument and recommendations; this will form the largest section of the report and will be divided into a logical sequence – by level of importance, or timescale, or whatever you decide
e present separately the appendices – statistical tables, drawings or plans, etc, referred to in the argument – in order not to deflect the reader from the main points of the report

4 Writing You will probably need to write at least two drafts of your report before you get it into an acceptable state. Remember:

- Keep to the subject; if something is not essential to your argument, however interesting or amusing, leave it out
- Make sure your facts and figures are correct
- Write simply in language that will be easy to understand
- Follow a logical pattern in your headings and argument
- Be positive, not negative – for example: 'It would be an advantage if . . .' rather than 'No advantage is achieved by . . .'
- If in difficulty over how to express what you mean, write something along the general lines. When you read it later, a better way of saying it will almost certainly occur to you; if you put nothing on paper you will have nothing to build on later
- Read through and correct your draft once or twice; do not continue to alter a word or phrase here and there for too long – there will never be the 'perfect' report and you must decide to stop rewriting before the whole exercise becomes tedious and what you gain by one amendment you lose elsewhere

'. . . do not continue to alter a word here and there – there will never be the "perfect" report . . .'

There follows an example of a very simple report requesting a certain course of action. You may feel that the result could have been achieved with less effort by going to see the man in charge and asking for a decision. The fact that you have taken the trouble to order your thoughts and present your argument on paper gives it extra weight and, if no action is taken on your suggestion at the time, at least there is a permanent record that you suggested it. As an example of a longer and more complicated 'report', the whole of this book can serve!

Report writing: a simple example

RXJ Manufacturing Ltd has three secretaries/shorthand-typists who were engaged to work for the three directors and undertake certain administrative tasks. The Managing Director's secretary is also the office manager or administrator, the Financial Director's secretary is also the wages clerk and cashier, and the Sales Director's secretary handles advertising and public relations, looks after the needs of the sales force and deals with quotations. The company has grown considerably over the past year or so and has taken on more staff — especially at middle management level. Apart from acquiring a telephonist/receptionist and a clerk, no extra administrative staff have been engaged and the three girls are finding that they are having to work long hours and are not doing their own jobs as well as they should because of the pressure of routine typing. All three grumble about the overload, but only you, the Sales Director's secretary, feel that the situation can be changed by positive action. The other girls have mentioned to you that they are seriously considering leaving for less exhausting jobs, but that if you can persuade the Managing Director that the expense of recruiting at least one more shorthand-typist is acceptable, they would be more than happy to stay.

Purpose: to achieve agreement to the recruitment of one extra shorthand-typist
To whom addressed: the Managing Director
Timescale: urgent

1 *Establish purpose and form* The purpose is clear; what facts can you bring to bear on its achievement? Write yourself a first draft of headings for argument. The company has grown and taken on more management, in other words, more originators of clerical and secretarial work. The secretaries, yourself included, like working for the company, but are unhappy with the overload and its result on their ability to do a really efficient job. A few facts and figures to give weight to this argument can easily be put together: number of extra hours worked by the three of you over the past four weeks, average workload for other managers handled in a day, for example. Explain your proposition for dealing with this, and how much it will cost. Compare this with the cost — and inconvenience — of losing the secretariat.

2 *Research and collation* Consult with the other girls and ask them to record the amount and general description of the work they do for other managers. Draw up a simple form similar to the one below. Ask them to recall the number of hours overtime they have worked over the past four weeks. Ask them for their recollection of any jobs which they have done poorly, any records they have allowed to fall behind, etc, because of the extra secretarial work.

Description	No of pages	Time taken	For whom
Reply to letter	1	10 min	Mr Smith
Quotation	4	50 min	Mr Jones
Report	6 (twice)	2 hours	Mr Smith
Arranging meeting	-	30 min	Mr Harrow

Make sure you have a list of the executives who have joined the company recently: compare the number of 'originators' to 'clerical workers'.

3 *Drafting* Having gathered your information you are now ready to draft the report as follows:

Title: Secretarial unrest and how to cure it
Introduction: explanation, purpose and conclusion
Argument: pros and cons of situation carefully presented in clear, unemotional terms
Appendices: figures to back up the argument

Fig 10 shows how your final report might look.

Dealing with the Press

As an executive secretary you may find yourself in the 'front-line' so far as dealing with the Press is concerned. If you are secretary to the Chairman or Marketing Director you may be considered, especially by the local Press, to be the prime source of authoritative information on the company you work for and its activities.

It is a good idea to foster and maintain a happy relationship with members of the Press – they can often be as useful to you as you can be to them in the exchange of information. Be very careful what you say to them, however. Be well briefed by your boss before you give *any* information to the Press and never, never make a statement 'off the record'. The need for confidentiality, so important in every aspect of the executive secretary's job, is that much more important when dealing with those not employed by the company.

Deal with requests for information promptly, even if you can only say that you have nothing to say! Never ignore a request by just not ringing back. This is no way to build up a good relationship. Make available adequate publicity material,

---

To: The Managing Director   Date

From: The secretariat

Subject: Secretarial unrest and how to cure it

The object of this report is to obtain permission to recruit one additional shorthand typist. We feel this is essential in order to:

(a) prevent the present secretarial staff leaving the company's employ

(b) provide the efficient service this company should give to its management and customers

Over the past year and a half the company has expanded rapidly. We have taken on the following middle management staff:

1 production manager
1 accountant
1 quality control manager
2 product managers
5 salespeople

Apart from a telephonist/receptionist (who does not type) and an accounts clerk, there has been no recruitment of office staff.

The secretariat is now over-extended and dissatisfied with the quality of service it can provide.

From Appendix A it will be seen that the extra hours worked over the past month alone amount to 118 - an average per secretary of 9.83 hours per week. This means that each of us has been working close to a six and a half day week. The four weeks taken as our base are typical of the amount of overtime that has been worked consistently for many months.

Appendix B shows three sample days (one from each of us) detailing the work, and time taken to complete it, that we have carried out in addition to our normal duties to the Directors. Appendix C contains copies of our job descriptions from which it will be clear that each of us has a full-time job without these extra duties.

This tremendous overload has not only caused unrest and unhappiness but, as shown in the examples given in Appendix D, consistent pressure and exhaustion have caused a number of errors, omissions and delays that can do the company no good.

With your permission and approval, we will advertise immediately to recruit a suitably experienced shorthand-typist. We suggest the costs would be in the order of:

Salary: circa £5000 pa
Equipment: typewriter £600
              chair £35
              desk - available spare in Drawing Office
Space: available in Sales Director's secretary's office
Instruction: the secretariat will be happy to undertake this

We feel that these costs compare well with the expense and inconvenience of replacing the experienced secretaries who make this request for help.

Attached

Appendix A: Schedule of overtime worked from 2 to 27 March
Appendix B: Details of extra work
Appendix C: Secretarial job descriptions (3)
Appendix D: Schedule of errors, omissions & delays

Fig 10 A simple report

pictures or samples as appropriate to the occasion. Accuracy is vital. Make sure you check your facts – and your boss's facts – before saying or writing anything for publication.

When issuing a Press release:

a be clear, concise and accurate
b provide back-up by way of photographs or brochures if possible
c ask your boss or another executive who may be more directly involved to check what you have written before you issue it
d send it only to those papers or journals you know will be interested

Recruitment of staff

The task of placing advertisements for staff required can become that of the executive secretary who works in a firm which is without a specialist concerned with recruitment. Apart from placing the advertisement, there are a number of ways in which you can take the opportunity to become involved in a wider and useful way.

Placing an advertisement

If you are asked to do this, first of all find out from the member of management concerned:

a details of the vacancy (job description, hours of work, salary to be offered and any other relevant information he can give you)
b the type of person ideally to be sought
c the papers or trade journals in which the advertisement should appear
d the amount of space to be reserved or money to be spent

Prepare a draft, based on this information, for approval or amendment and then contact the chosen newspapers or journals to place the advertisement. If time is short this can be arranged over the telephone, but to be sure of the correct result it is advisable to send written confirmation. Remember to ask for a copy or copies of the paper or journal in which the advertisement appears to be sent to you.

The form your advertisement takes will depend on the seniority of the vacancy offered. The recruitment of a member of the management team will probably merit an expensive 'display' of about 10 cm depth across two columns or even more, whereas for a junior clerk, four or five lines in one column will suffice. For the management position, the national daily papers and the appropriate trade journals will be used; for the junior, the local paper will be more appropriate, together with sending details to the local Job Centre or employment office. If you are responsible for advertising for staff as a rule, you will very quickly learn the most effective way of phrasing advertisements and the best periodicals in which to place them to get a satisfactory response.

When composing your advertisement, bring out the favourable aspects of the job, but remember – particularly for the more junior posts – to mention any facts that might rule out certain applicants, such as the need for own transport, considerable overtime to be worked, working away from home, a 'no smoking' rule. If your company has a salary scale, mention the rates offered; if not, agree with the manager of the department concerned a median figure which can be given as a guideline. Paint a truthful picture of the position on offer. This, together with the approximate salary the position carries, will save a lot of candidates from applying for a job which they would find unsuitable. Figs 11 and 12 show examples of the two types of advertisement.

ENGINEERING MANAGER: We are a subtantial privately owned food processing Group in a pleasant location and need an Engineering Manager to join our young management team.

Candidates should have formal mechanical or electrical engineering qualifications (preferably to Degree standard) and several years' management experience. Some knowledge of food technology would be an advantage.

The successful candidate will report to our Group Managing Director. He/she will be responsible for all mechanical and electrical installation and maintenance, building construction, transport services and will control a staff of 30+.

The Group operates an excellent pension/life assurance scheme and offers free private health insurance cover. The salary will be in the region of £.. ...pa plus a 2-litre company car.
Please apply in writing, giving details of qualifications and experience to ...

Fig 11 Display advertisement

JUNIOR CLERK. Due to promotion we need a junior clerk in our computerised wages office. No experience necessary. Pay is about £.. a week and we have a subsidised cafeteria. Applicants aged 16/17, prepared not to smoke in the office, keen to learn and help out with general duties should telephone Ms ... of ... Ltd on 006 008090 for an application form.

Fig 12 Single column advertisement

Giving recruitment assistance

Your connection with recruitment could end here. However, if this aspect of personnel work appeals to you then you can undoubtedly be of enormous help to any member of the management who is seeking staff. If the vacancy is a junior one, you may be asked to conduct the initial screening interview, but the final choice will rest with the senior person in the department where the vacancy exists.

Whatever the vacancy and whoever is to conduct the interview, your sensible planning and preparation will smooth the way. Be prepared for the replies to the advertisement by setting up three separate files of classification:

To be interviewed
Possible
Unsuitable

As the replies come in (either completed application forms you have sent to the juniors who telephoned or the letters and career details sent by the prospective Engineering Managers) you will read each one very carefully, at least twice, in order to decide the category in which to place it. Type a list of the names and addresses of *all* the applicants and keep this on file for future reference.

The senior position
Write a short summary of the application for the post of Engineering Manager and pin this to the front of each of the letters in the first category. If the Managing Director (and any other senior person concerned with the selection) agrees to interview those you have chosen, this summary can then be used at the interview. Here is an example of a summary:

```
Candidate for interview: (name)   Interview date: (time and date)

Address:                          Married:

Telephone no:                     Children:

Need to relocate:

Qualifications:   (degree, diploma, professional association
                   membership, etc)

Work experience: (position and company)

Comments at interview:

(This can include headings such as: knowledge of workfield,
drive & initiative, personality, appearance, conversational
ability, and so on.)
```

A number of firms produce preprinted interview forms with boxes to tick according to the degree of each skill or quality possessed and these can save you a little time and effort if the interviewer likes the idea. It is a simple task, however, for you to prepare your own form on the lines of the example above and photocopy it for the completion of details taken by you from each original letter of application.

For senior vacancies, it is often the case that the Managing Director will want other directors or senior managers present at the initial interview. Once the decision has been made about who to invite for interview, photocopy all the details for each candidate chosen and distribute them in good time for the interviewers concerned to make a reasonable assessment.

Having received the Managing Director's decision, you can now arrange the interviews for those selected and write the letters to applicants not selected. If you can contact the interview candidates by telephone (preferably at home in the evening rather than at their workplace) so much the better, because you can agree on a time and date in one operation rather than offering an appointment by letter, when the date suggested may not be suitable. Describe the location of your premises and send a copy map of the area when you write to confirm the interview details.

The best of the 'possibles' (which the Managing Director will indicate) should be sent a holding letter saying that the selection of interview candidates has not been completed and that you will contact them again shortly. This will probably be a negative answer in due course, but sometimes those candidates interviewed in the first place do not come up to expectations or do not accept the job when offered it, and so keeping contact open with the borderline candidates is sensible.

The remainder of the 'possibles' and the 'unsuitables' should receive a prompt and courteous reply to their applications. Something along the lines of:

Thank you for your letter of application for the position as Engineering Manager with our Group.

We have received an enormous response to our advertisement, mostly from highly qualified engineers already working in the food processing industry. We have therefore decided to interview only those candidates whose background experience most closely corresponds with our particular needs.

May we nonetheless thank you for applying to us and wish you every success in the future.

The interviews The first interviews have been arranged, you have told Reception who to expect and when, and all managers concerned have received copies of the candidates' details.

For senior positions it is useful to provide the candidate with a copy of the job description of the vacant position and to give him the necessary time to read and absorb it before he is interviewed. He can do this in your office (possibly with a cup of tea or coffee if he wishes). Reading through the job description not only tells the applicant what he will be responsible for and expected to do, but gives him the basis for asking questions about the job at the interview. Invite him to take a copy of the job description away with him when he leaves. Re-reading it at home will help him to decide whether he wants the job if it is offered to him.

After these initial interviews, there will be time for consultation and decision making about who to put on the shortlist for a final interview. The number of applicants shortlisted is usually small, sometimes only two or three, and this second interview is one where time has to be given for the candidates to look around the premises, meet their prospective colleagues, and ask and be asked searching questions. Here you may be involved in planning the itinerary for the tour of the premises and the introductions to members of staff the successful candidate will be working with. It might be worth suggesting to the interviewer(s) that questions about actual situations within the sphere of operation be asked of the candidate at this interview. Together with the interviewer with whom the final decision will rest, you can formulate a few questions giving the background to the situation and relevant facts. The candidates will then be asked '... and how would you deal with this ...' or '... how would you approach this problem ...'

After the decision has been made, all that remains for you to do is to tie up the loose ends by writing again to the possibles, to the unsuccessful interview candidates and to the person who is to be offered the job. The successful candidate's letter confirming his appointment will be a formal one from the Managing Director and will include the company's terms of employment, rate of salary agreed, pension scheme rules, holiday and sickness leave entitlement, etc. It could also include an expression of pleasure at the appointment and belief that the candidate will be happy and successful in the job.

Send a memorandum to all senior management confirming the appointment of the new Engineering Manager, giving a few details of his background, qualifications and experience. Notices should be displayed on boards giving the new manager's name and starting date so that *all* employees know of the change.

Junior appointments
For junior staff less preparatory work is necessary as the application forms will present all the details and the manager interviewing the candidates will not need a précis from you. Nor is more than one interview usually needed to make a decision. At the interviews a general discussion of the applicants' back-

ground, school successes, hobbies and interests will put them at their ease and let the interviewer find out something of their personalities. It is useful to have a simple task or two for the applicants to perform so that an idea of their approach to work can be gained and a few questions can be asked based on the job they will be doing, if they are successful.

In each individual case of recruitment of staff, you will learn as you go how you can be of maximum assistance and where your particular talents can be put to best use.

Supervision, delegation and motivation

In many executive secretarial positions you will be responsible for a junior secretary who will work with you, and the ability to choose appropriate work to delegate to her will be one of your responsibilities. Don't expect her to deal with difficult problems; you are there to do that. She is there to learn from you and to lessen your workload on routine tasks. Explain carefully each job you give her to do and make it plain to her that you would prefer she ask questions – many times over if necessary – rather than guess at things she has not grasped.

Try to get her interested and enthusiastic about learning from you and developing a professional approach to her work. You may find yourself with a high-flyer who will learn quickly and be off to better things in a very short time, or you may have someone working with you who will never want the responsibility of a really senior job. In either case, do not keep your junior with you longer than is right for *her*. Once she is competent to stand in for you in your absence and has learned the essentials of working as a secretary (rather than just improving her shorthand and typewriting) encourage her to apply for a job of her own. If she is not set on a career, you should nevertheless try to persuade her that working without your supervision as, say, secretary to a middle-manager, will be more satisfying for her than remaining under your wing for years. This may be hard for you to do because, of course, she is now your 'right-hand' and can do many jobs without your supervision.

The thought of starting from scratch with yet another school leaver may depress you, but part of your job has been to teach, and if you have taught well by example and demonstration, she should move on; if not to further a career, then simply for the opportunity to learn to do something different – and to be responsible for her own work. If she is really competent it might be logical for her to take over from you at some stage but, of course, this will depend on your own satisfaction in your job; whether your areas of 'own responsibility' are growing and extending your abilities.

You may also in some positions have overall responsibility for a typing pool – usually not more than four or five typists, otherwise it tends to become a full-time supervisor's job. Your aim must be to motivate (in other words enthuse) your staff in the work they have to do. This will not be an easy task, because working in a typing pool can become a dreary treadmill with very little involvement by the typists with the work they type. They will probably each be typing for any or all managers and junior executives who do not have a secretary of their own and there will be little continuity of work content for the girls. One may start dealing with the correspondence for a certain job, another may get the next stage of it and yet another continue with the final stages. If work can be organised in such a way that each girl deals with the same manager's work and can see the 'sense' of what she is doing, more identification with the job can be achieved. This is something that you, as the supervisor, will need to try to organise depending on the type of business you are in and the number of originators of work and typing staff employed. It needs careful thought, time and common sense on your part.

On a day to day basis you will need to monitor incoming and outgoing work for the section. You should request that all originators' work comes through you to the typists. You can then make sure that urgent work is dealt with first and that routine work gets done in good time and in the order in which it is given to you. Check several times during the day that the work flow is reasonable and that no one typist (possibly because she happens to be the most efficient) is being overloaded while another is idle.

Try to establish the preferences of each girl for the sort of work she does and, as far as possible, arrange that she gets that kind of work. (There are some typists who genuinely enjoy typing figures!) Until you can rely absolutely on the abilities of the girls to check and correct their own (or each other's) work, read through everything that is typed before it is collected by the originator. Always be fair and consistent in your attitudes and comments and always be ready to help with queries about the work.

Liaise between the typists and the executives they work for and sort out difficulties that may arise between them. Defend the typists' right to fair and sensible treatment from the executives, and the executives' right to expect correct and speedy work from the typists. Your position as middleman is one that needs initiative and tact, because you must not be directly identified with either management or typing pool. You should persuade both groups to bring any complaints to you for arbitration. Aim to get both groups to have consideration for the other's problems, to avoid the 'them and us' attitude and to work as a team whose end product is helping the company to be successful.

Further education and training

If you have young and relatively untrained staff, you should encourage them to continue with their studies. Be seen to be interested in their progress, concerned with their improvement and promotion prospects. There are evening classes and day-release facilities run by local education authorities, providing courses leading to the Pitman Examinations Institute and London Chamber of Commerce and Industry certificates in secretarial studies.

If *you* have not already gained a Private Secretary's Certificate or Diploma, consider working for one. Studying for and passing examinations at this advanced level will prove to your employer that you are keen to learn, encourage your subordinates in their own studies and give you an excellent recommendation for securing a top job when you decide to move on. Once you hold such a certificate or diploma, you can join the Institute of Qualified Private Secretaries, and this will open up further avenues for learning by receiving their journal and attending their local and national meetings.

Many professional bodies, including the British Institute of Management and the Industrial Society, now see the sense of operating short courses for secretarial staff. These range from basic lectures and discussion groups for more junior staff to three or four day residential seminars for senior executive secretaries. As well as encouraging staff who report to you to participate, it is well worth going along yourself to a seminar, even if you already have a Diploma, not only to listen to what the lecturers have to say, but to exchange views and ideas with the other senior secretaries attending so that you can broaden your view and refresh your approach.

Delegating

When you delegate a job to your subordinates you should:

a enthuse them for your purpose by explaining it clearly
b tell them why you want them to do it
c instruct them in how to make a start
d explain to them (if this applies) the interim stages and broadly how you see each stage developing
e keep them informed of overall progress regularly
f praise them for effort and achievement
g if you have to criticise anything explain why you think they are wrong and suggest ways of improvement

Praise works better than criticism and it is always possible to find something of value in anyone. If you can build confidence you can improve performance. Many people are 'failures' through lack of confidence. A person's self esteem is a product of their treatment by others throughout life. If someone who works for you has suffered from over-critical companions, family or employers, you will have to work extra hard to find what is praiseworthy in them. The earlier in a relationship you can begin to build a person's self confidence the better.

When you have to criticise, it *must* be fair criticism. Your subordinates must know what you have set as their targets for achievement and you must have explained – and explained again if necessary – what you want them to do, how you want it done and by when. If you know that you did all these things to the best of your ability and they have still made a mess of it, then you will have to criticise. Try to leave the person with something to build on; shortcomings and mistakes must be pointed out with helpful, constructive recommendations for improvement given. You should never leave subordinates feeling that they have failed hopelessly and are totally incompetent. Rather, they should feel that they can improve, and have positive plans for doing so.

At all times you must be fair and consistent with your subordinates. They need to recognise that they can trust you completely and rely on your word. Promises must be honoured. If, through circumstances beyond your control, they have to be broken or deferred, be sure to explain exactly why this is and what you propose to do instead.

Letting go

'What man can conceive – man can achieve.' (Jules Verne)
'but not necessarily single-handed!' (Philippa Ramage)

In each particular executive secretary's job there will be many differing areas of 'own responsibility'. These are too wide and varied to deal with in this book, but if you have confidence in your abilities you will be able and willing to accept the challenge of organising and controlling them on your own. Being directly concerned in a variety of areas in the business you work for will add enormously to your job satisfaction. However, do not allow yourself to become swamped with too many additional responsibilities. If they grow so numerous and diverse that they prevent you doing your main job (which is to provide an excellent secretarial service to your boss), then some of these extra tasks will have to be passed on to others. If you are genuinely becoming overburdened by these responsibilities, you must say so before they damage your abilities as a secretary.

Never think that no one else can do a job as well as you can. Be ready to 'let go' certain areas of control. Always remember that your prime purpose is to provide a support system for your boss – but that you do not necessarily have to do that without help from others!

Summary

- Organise your time and work around your routine for the day
- Look at tomorrow's schedule (preferably with your boss) before you leave each day and make sure your diaries correspond
- Refer to the diary and 'bring-forward' system regularly and often
- Know your sources of information – inside and outside the office
- 'Social' aspects: establish contacts with reliable suppliers; find out from your boss what his preferences are; learn all you can from the 'experts'
- When writing a report remember its purpose, who is to receive it and the deadline; keep to the subject and research supportive evidence carefully; correct and amend your draft, but know when to stop – there is no 'perfect' report
- In dealing with the Press: establish good relationships with individuals; be accurate (check with your boss), concise and helpful; never make an 'off the record' statement
- Recruitment of staff: make sure you know what is offered, the ideal person to be sought, where to advertise and how much to spend; look for ways in which you can assist the interviewer; be organised, prompt in your replies and considerate in your letters of rejection
- Nurture your subordinates by being consistent in your attitude and fair in your decisions; patient with their need to ask questions; constructive in your criticism; encouraging to them on further education and training – especially by demonstrating your own interest in becoming better qualified
- Recognise when any extra responsibilities are becoming damaging to your ability to provide a first class secretarial service to your boss; know when to 'let go' – be confident enough to seek support from others

6 Meetings

Before the meeting: convening, agenda and preparation

Convening

The duties of a secretary begin with the convening of the meeting. If there are a large number of people involved, this will take a lot of time in telephoning those concerned (or their secretaries) to ensure that they are free to attend. Agree with your boss on a number of possible dates and times to give a better chance of getting everyone to come, and make sure you know who *must* be there so that you can telephone them first. For a meeting of ten people you may have to make dozens of telephone calls. If your boss is the Chairman and/or Managing Director your problem will be lessened in that many of those invited to attend will rearrange their plans in order to be available. If the meeting is a regular one on a prearranged day of the month, you will need only to send out the agenda in good time to ensure the attendance of all members. To arrange an ad hoc meeting of more than, say, three people will take time and patience, however. If time permits and there is no agenda to be issued in advance of the meeting, send out a memo or letter confirming the time, date and place and the purpose of the meeting.

Agenda

Some days before the meeting is to take place, your boss will have given you the items he wishes to put on the agenda and told you who else to ask for other items. You will have brought forward items from the previous meeting as indicated by the minutes. You will either present a draft of the agenda to your boss for his revision, or, once you are established in your job and he feels it appropriate, he will leave the entire preparation to you. Make sure you note on the agenda the people concerned with each item and any papers attached or previously circulated. In pencil on the chairman's agenda, note anything he particularly wants to raise and discuss.

Preparation

Reserve the meeting room in good time and organise coffee, tea or lunch to be served as appropriate. If the meeting is to go on through lunchtime you will probably be the one required to provide sandwiches or a buffet. The arrangements for these will be your responsibility, and quite possibly the serving or even the making of them too.

Immediately before the meeting make sure that the room to be used is set out with sufficient chairs, paper, pens or pencils, carafes of drinking water and glasses, together with any visual aids necessary. If the meeting is to take place in your boss's office, clear his desk of all other papers.

The chairman's meeting file will have the annotated agenda and the minutes of the previous meeting, together with any previously circulated papers. The secretary will take with her the Minute Book containing the agreed minutes of previous meetings, an attendance register to be signed by all those attending the meeting, a file similar to the chairman's for her own use (plus a few spare copies of the agenda, last meeting's minutes and previously circulated papers just in case any member has neglected to bring his own), a shorthand notebook and her own pencils or pens.

During the meeting: the secretary's role

The decision as to who writes the minutes (or notes) of a meeting is up to the chairman of each particular meeting (except in the case of Annual General Meetings or Extraordinary General Meetings, where the Company Secretary is responsible). At regular meetings of the board of directors the meeting secretary can be the Company Secretary or the Chairman's private secretary or even the Company Secretary's secretary. This may sound confusing, but in practice it tends to be simplified by a process of elimination – whoever is best qualified to write minutes tends to get the job! Throughout this chapter, it is assumed that you are the secretary to the meeting chairman.

If you find yourself with the duty to report a meeting which follows a formal pattern where motions are proposed, have to be seconded and voted on, then you should read the appropriate sections of books dealing with this subject (many secretarial handbooks contain such information). You can also learn from reading the minutes of previous meetings and, at the first few meetings you attend as secretary, ask the chairman to indicate to you how you should be recording each minute. You will not be expected to undertake this task unaided in the initial stages and the chairman will guide you through your first few meetings.

For the most part, the executive secretary will be required to minute rather less formal meetings and the example given in this chapter does not include formalities. No special 'meeting' language is necessary and the minutes produced are simply a record of suggestions, views, agreement and action to be taken by those attending.

Always try to persuade your boss to allow you to be present at the meetings of which you are to type the minutes. Sometimes, directors feel that they are better able to take notes at the time and then dictate the finished minutes to their secretaries. This takes all the fun out of typing minutes for the secretary and distances her from the heart of the business. The argument is sometimes put that the executives or directors will feel some restraint in what they discuss if a secretary is present but this is not usually so. After a very short time, the secretary at the meeting does seem to become 'one of them' – or it could be that she simply fades into the background very well! Of course, the major argument in favour of a secretary actually attending the meeting is that it relieves her boss of what can be, to him, the tiresome task of gathering and dictating an accurate record from his notes.

In most cases the minutes of the previous meeting will be taken as read and are simply agreed as an accurate record. Occasionally there will be a correction to be made. This will be recorded by the secretary and included as a first item in the minutes of that meeting.

The chairman will then ask for matters arising from the last meeting. These may be deferred until later if the agenda includes another item which relates to them. If there is no such later item, they will be discussed at this point.

The chairman will ask the individual named beside each item on the agenda in turn for comment and general discussion of each point will follow. The term 'general discussion' covers a multitude of conditions! There may be disagreement and even violent argument. What happens at a meeting is not necessarily what is minuted. You must concentrate on the essentials; note points raised, action to be taken and conclusions reached.

At meetings you attend in order to take notes or minutes there are a number of points to bear in mind. The minutes of a meeting are not a verbatim record; a two hour meeting may well produce only one A4 sheet of minutes. Be brief, but be sure you do not miss any items of importance and decision. You must remember that you are a part of the meeting only in your capacity as a record keeper. You are *not* required to comment or direct the meeting in any way whatsoever. You speak only when directly addressed, and this will probably be on a matter of checking dates or referring to past papers or reading back an item previously minuted. It can be difficult for a secretary to remain silent in some meetings, but in formal circumstances, eg a board meeting, you must do so. In informal meetings this is not an absolute rule but, even so, you should wait until you are asked for an opinion before giving it.

With a good chairman the meeting will proceed through the

agenda efficiently, with enough time being allowed for the various items to be discussed, members of the meeting being tactfully kept to the subject and action indicated before moving on to the next item. The chairman will, in other words, 'control' the meeting and will often indicate to the secretary what should and should not be minuted. However, chairmen have been known to allow a meeting to degenerate into a 'free for all', when items will be raised out of order and members will depart from the subject and ramble on at length. There is nothing a secretary can do about this at the meeting and all her wits will be needed to make sense of her notes and decide what should be recorded – as well as keeping her impatience to herself. If you always write the minutes for particular meetings you will soon become adjusted to the pattern they follow and will be able to make sense of what at first may appear to be a total jumble of information.

'Chairmen have been known to allow a meeting to degenerate into a "free for all" . . .'

After the meeting: minutes, action list, and taking action

It is vital to transcribe the notes as soon as possible after you leave the meeting. Clear away the debris and tidy the meeting room first; deal with any urgent messages that have been left for you in your absence and then begin on the minutes. Type a first draft for your own revision; a second draft for your boss's comments and revision (if this is still a relatively new job for you – in due course this will not be necessary); and finally a fair copy for duplication and circulation to the members of the meeting and others who need to be informed.

'... after the meeting clear away the debris ...'

The sooner after a meeting the minutes are received, the sooner the members are reminded of things that they have undertaken to do. While many people make notes of what suggestions and instructions were given during a meeting, there are times when they are not quite clear on exactly what they agreed to do, or when. It is sometimes the practice to leave a wide margin on the right-hand side of the final copy of the minutes and to note the names or initials of the people who are to take action. Underline or highlight on each individual's copy where their name appears in order to draw their attention quickly to parts of the minutes which directly concern them.

You will be able to follow the pattern set in the writing of minutes before you joined the company or, if you consider that they have not been well written, you can in the early stages of this job, discuss this with your boss when you present your first draft and ask for his views on how he would like to see the meeting minuted. Once a good working relationship has been established between the meeting chairman and the secretary it may also be possible for you to give a little help in controlling the meeting – outside the meeting of course! For example, you could note on the chairman's copy of the agenda a suggested time allowance for each item and any background information you have on each subject. The organising of a productive meeting is very much a partnership between the chairman and the secretary, and the secretary can be of enormous help behind the scenes.

When you type your first draft of the minutes, make an action list for yourself. If you read through the specimen minutes in this chapter, you will see that a number of items require action on the part of the secretary: meetings to arrange, a memo to be written, an evening appointment to be fixed (and a speech to be composed by the chairman which will require the secretary's help). These are apart from the normal follow-up items to be dealt with before the next meeting. You will also have all the papers circulated before and during the meeting to file in the appropriate places and possibly graphs or charts to update with figures supplied to the meeting. In the day following a meeting which you attended and minuted, you will be very well occupied.

When you compile the agenda for the next meeting and telephone each person who may have an item for inclusion, take the opportunity to remind them again of any action they undertook at the last meeting to carry out. This will be useful to them and will keep you in touch with what has happened; being aware of the current situation makes your job more interesting and ensures that you are well informed if your boss asks you what is happening in any area of operation.

An example of a meeting

This is a regular weekly management meeting. Study the specimen agenda in Fig 13 on page 90.

Items to be raised are listed in the order decided by the chairman or by precedent. Alongside these may be given the name of the principal speaker responsible and mention of papers previously circulated or to be presented at the meeting.

On the chairman's copy it is a useful practice to make notes of any points he wants to make or questions he needs to ask. It is, of course, essential that all relevant paperwork is placed in his meeting file in order of discussion.

This was what took place at the meeting:

Dr Fairbairne (as usual) delayed the start of the meeting by being late and having to be summoned from the laboratory. Mr Avison was (as usual) irritated by this lateness.

The chairman called the meeting to order and was told by Heather Linley that her boss, Peter King, had been involved in a car accident the previous evening but was not badly hurt and had telephoned to ask her to stand in at his part of the meeting. A considerable amount of chat ensued – with some acrid comments by Avison on the dangers of drinking and driving, and keen defence of Peter King by everyone else – including, especially,

```
                        MANAGEMENT MEETING
    to be held on Monday June 7 198- at 10.00 am in the
                office of the Managing Director
    ----------------------------------------------------

                            A G E N D A

    1.    Minutes of the meeting held on May 30 198-
          (previously circulated)

    2.    Matters arising

    3.    Manufacturing:  Mr Keith Avison (paper to be presented)

    4.    Technical development: Dr Charles Fairbairne

    5.    Sales and marketing:  Mr Peter King (UK)
                                Mr Marcus Welsh (Overseas)

    6.    Advertising and public relations:  Miss Jane Smith

    7.    Personnel:  Mrs Claire Wells

    8.    Finance:  Mr John Routh (paper on budget control
          previously circulated)

    9.    Any other business

    10.   Date of next meeting

    ----------------------------------------------------
```

Fig 13 A specimen agenda

his secretary. The meeting then came to order and started to deal with the real business on the agenda. Had a verbatim record been kept it would have been as follows:

Minutes

John Routh: I see there is an error in the minutes – not a big one but nonetheless I like to see an accurate record. I don't remember anything being 'agreed' about a visit to Nigeria for Marcus – I think it would be better to say 'proposed'. After all, we are still nowhere near a decision that we should spend all that money on sorting things out there.
(Groans all round)

Chairman: Will everyone please amend the minutes of the last meeting accordingly.

Matters arising

Dr Fairbairne: B... all seems to have been done in the machine shop to house my new assembly. How long am I supposed to wait this time to get a new piece of machinery installed? After all, I'm not asking them to build the damn thing – just find a few square feet to drop it in.

Mr Avison:	Now, Charlie – Rome wasn't built in a day, you know. (Dr F hates being called 'Charlie' and equally hates truisms like this – and Mr A knows it.) I was asked only last week to make the space available and as everyone knows there is precious little space to be made available – Charlie's newfangled contraptions are taking up most of the shop floor already.
Dr F:	If it was left to you, Keith, we'd still be using donkeys and wheels to generate power.
Mr A:	Don't worry lad, you'll have your space by next week . . . even if it means some of my men'll have to shift their machines out the back door.
Chairman:	Yes, well . . . I'm sure it won't quite come to that. Perhaps you'd let Charles know as soon as you have a suitable space?
Mr A:	Aye, well, as I said, it isn't as though we've got nowt else to do but shove machines about for space for experiments . . .
Chairman:	(cutting him short) Nevertheless . . .
Mr A:	Aye – right.
Mr Welsh:	I want to settle this point about the trip to Nigeria – proposed or agreed. I need to know whether I can go because they seem to have made a complete foul-up out there and someone's got to talk sense to them before the whole thing falls flat on its face.
Chairman:	Mark, I do agree to your going, but let's talk about it later in the meeting, under Overseas sales. I'd like to consider the manufacturing report from Keith now because it doesn't look too healthy to me from a quick glance at his last week's figures here.

Manufacturing

Mr A:	Aye, well – it has dropped a bit because some of the chaps are already on holiday and we've had a few difficulties, what with trying to find extra space for experimental machines and all.
Chairman:	How many men short are you?
Mr A:	Three last week and five this – and it'll be four or five for some time now – on through July and August anyway, so I'll be taking on some casual labour . . . if that's agreed?
Chairman:	Yes certainly, but that does bring us to this vexed question of a fixed factory closure. We've discussed it in previous years and not managed to reach agreement. More and more firms are closing for a couple of weeks in the summer and

	it does enable production for the rest of the time to be kept pretty stable.
Mr A:	I've always been for it, as you know. It's just that it's difficult to persuade chaps they've got no choice as to when they can take their time off in the summer and those without kids don't want to be stuck with August when the mobs go.
Mrs Wells:	I don't think it would be too difficult to arrange. It would, of course, leave people with only five other days after that – and we had thought of shutting for the whole of the Christmas week which would erode even that short time. It is time-wasting for the men to have to teach the casual labourers how to do things. A lot of them think it's more trouble than it's worth and would rather do overtime and earn a bit more money.
Chairman:	Look, I think we need to go into this very thoroughly and come to a decision in good time to make it clear for next year. Could we all get together just to thrash out this one question and formulate a definite policy on holidays?
	(General nodding and agreement)
	Right, Jean, fix that up will you – soon as you can? Any other problems, Keith?
Mr A:	No, that's my lot.
Chairman:	OK. Charles – what have you got?
Dr F:	What do you think of my report on the new circuits?
Chairman:	Excellent – most encouraging. What's it going to cost to put into operation?
Dr F:	Oh, I don't think it'll break the bank, but quite honestly I haven't got around to thinking in fiscal terms. I was so damned pleased to solve the problem at last.
Mr Routh:	Well, from a few rough calculations made since I got the report yesterday, it looks perfectly reasonable – in fiscal terms, as you say, Charles.
Mr A:	I don't know about fiscal terms – I suppose you money men will juggle it somehow – but I don't look forward to more b. . . . .ing about on the shop floor. I've had one b. . . .y invention after another lately and half of them come to nothing after all the inconvenience and loss of production they cause.
Chairman:	Now, Keith, give this one a fair chance. I'd like John to do a detailed costing in liaison with you and Charles. Will you do that, John – soon as you can?
	(Nods from JR, CF and a grunt from KA)

Mrs Wells:	One point that strikes me, Mr Chairman, is that if we do use these new electronics, would we be likely to have redundancies?
Mr A:	Aye, well ... I'm not having any redundancies. None of that 'made by robots' in my shop, I can tell you.
Chairman:	Let's leave it until we see what it's going to cost – we'll talk about it next Monday. John, can you get the figures out by then, do you think?
Mr R:	Should be possible, yes.
Chairman:	Fine, that's excellent. So let's have a look at the UK sales figures shall we, Heather?

And so it went on – argument and disagreement, asides which had nothing to do with the point, personal prejudices on display at every turn. If you compare the first four items on the agenda covered by the verbatim record with the suggested written minutes below (Fig 14), you will see that it is quite simple to leave out what has no bearing on the case and to phrase comments made in such a way that nothing essential is lost. These example minutes are quite detailed and, depending on the chairman's wishes, they could show only decisions taken and who is to action them. As an exercise, go through the minutes given here and rewrite them in the shortest possible way, remembering to leave out nothing valid.

MINUTES of the MANAGEMENT MEETING held on MONDAY JUNE 7 198-

   Present: Mr Guy Bolding, Managing Director (in the chair)
              Mr Keith Avison, Production Manager
              Dr Charles Fairbairne, Technical Director
              Mr John Routh, Financial Director
              Miss Jane Smith, Advertising Manager
              Mrs Claire Wells, Personnel Officer
              Mr Marcus Welsh, Sales Director: Overseas
              Miss Heather Linley (secretary to Mr Peter King)

              Miss Jean Brown   (in attendance)

   Apologies for absence were received from Mr Peter King, Sales Director UK, who had been slightly injured in a motor accident.

1. Minutes

   The minutes of the meeting held on May 30 were agreed as an accurate record, with the exception of the following:

   (9) Any other business: (ii) Visit to Nigeria - delete 'agreed to make' and subsititue 'proposed to make'.

   After this amendment had been made, the Chairman signed the minutes as correct.

2. Matters arising   Action

   (i) Dr Fairbairne asked what action had been taken by Manufacturing following his suggestion for a rearrangement of plant in the factory to accommodate his new valve assembly. He had been in the machine shop earlier that morning and had seen no evidence of any change.
   Mr Avison replied that the matter was in hand and should be completed by the beginning of next week. The Chairman suggested that Mr Avison let Dr Fairbairne know immediately the assembly was installed.   KA

   (ii) Mr Welsh referred to the proposed Nigerian trip and the Chairman requested that this item be deferred for discussion under item 5 - Overseas sales and marketing.

3. Manufacturing

   Mr Avison distributed the weekly manufacturing report and apologised for a drop in output. This was due to the holiday period having begun. He asked if it would be possible to take on casual labour to compensate in some part for these absences, which would be increasing over the next two months. The Chairman agreed to this request but felt that a decision must shortly be taken on the subject of complete factory closure for two weeks in the summer in future years so that it would not be necessary to engage casual workers. The Chairman asked the secretary to arrange a meeting of all departmental heads to discuss this subject specifically. JB

4. Technical development

   Dr Fairbairne asked for comments on his previously circulated report dealing with the breakthrough made in electronic circuitry. The Chairman said he had found it most encouraging and asked Mr Routh to collaborate with Dr Fairbairne and Mr Avison on producing a more detailed costing for its utilisation. KA/CF/JR

   Mr Avison felt that unless a substantial saving could be achieved there seemed little point in more upheaval in manufacturing.

   Mrs Wells expressed some apprehension over the possibility of job redundancies.

   The Chairman suggested that further discussion should be left until the detailed costings had been produced and this item was deferred until the next meeting of the management team.

5. Sales and marketing

   United Kingdom: Miss Heather Linley (secretary to Mr King) passed round copies of the weekly sales figures and drew attention to the lack of availability from Manufacturing of Line 24B. Mr Avison agreed to look into this. It was noted that once again Northern Division representatives had exceeded their target by a substantial margin and the Chairman said he would write a congratulatory memorandum. He asked whether Mr King would shortly be back at work and Miss Linley replied that she had heard just before the meeting of his hope to return by Thursday or Friday this week (June 10/11). KA

   GB

   Overseas: Mr Welsh referred to the previously circulated sales figures and said that it appeared vital that he visit Nigeria to sort out difficulties there. The Chairman agreed and asked Mr Welsh to remain after the close of the meeting to finalise arrangements.

   European sales continued to improve, although slowly, and Mr Welsh wondered if a little more money could be allocated for advertising in this area. Miss Jane Smith said that the budget did not allow for any further monies for Europe but that possibly some adjustment could be made in the next financial year. Mr Routh agreed to consider this suggestion well in advance of the new financial year beginning on October 1 and said that his draft budget figures would be available for discussion in two weeks' time. JR

6. Advertising and public relations

   Miss Jane Smith said that the television campaign had proved an enormous success in the north of England - as witness the increase in sales - and that she would now like to go nationwide. The Chairman said he would need time to consider this proposal in the light of the need to export more. He agreed to discuss Miss Smith's proposals at a meeting to be arranged in the near future. GB/JS

   (At this point, the Chairman thanked Miss Linley for her attendance and she returned to her office.)

7. Personnel

   Mrs Wells began by asking that she be allowed to bring to the proposed meeting regarding a factory close-down for holidays next year certain supervisory staff from the shop floor. This was welcomed and agreed. The Chairman also requested that she might care to do a little research into the possible reactions of all staff to the suggestion of a fixed holiday period before the meeting was convened.

   The Chairman asked if any further moves had been apparent towards full unionisation in the factory. Mrs wells said that she felt it would inevitably come but that no definite agreement had been reached. Mr Avison felt that many workers were not keen to join a union and there was only a small minority move in that direction. Both he and Mrs Wells were keeping a close watch on developments.

Mr Avison requested special permission for a six-week leave of absence for a machine shop worker with ten years' service. His wife was to have a major operation and the employee needed the time off to look after her and their children. The Chairman agreed to this request but suggested that only a portion of this time, possibly half, should be at full pay. Mrs Wells said she would find out what precedent had been set in the company and would consult the rules which applied throughout industry.

CW

8. Finance

Mr Routh pointed out that in several areas budgets had already been exceeded. He felt it unnecessary to go through the figures item by item at this meeting. All those concerned had received copies of his directive on the subject of adhering to budgets. He was disappointed by this overspending and, if the company was to increase its profits over the last year, very little could be spent between now and the end of September.

General discussion followed but it was finally agreed that cutbacks would be made so far as was possible. The Chairman felt that this year's target had proved somewhat unrealistic and looked forward to discussion of draft budgets for next year in two weeks' time. He asked Mr Routh to let him have a copy of the draft as soon as it was prepared.

JR

9. Any other business

Mr Routh asked the Chairman if it would be in order to arrange a farewell dinner for the Senior Accountant who was due to retire early because of ill health. He was 59 and had been with the company since its formation 30 years ago. The Chairman agreed. Mr Routh then asked if the Chairman would be prepared to make a speech of appreciation and presentation at the dinner. The Chairman said he would be delighted to make the presentation and Mr Routh was asked to arrange a suitable date with Miss Brown.

GB/JR/CB

10. Date of next meeting: Monday June 14 at 10.00 am

Fig 14 Specimen minutes

Action list

When you read through your first draft of the minutes, note down in the order in which it appears any action needed by you. Then sort the items into sections. From the minutes given as an example your action list would look something like this:

Diary:
1. Dept heads (+ supervisors) meeting re fixed holidays
2. Jane Smith/GB re nationwide TV advertising
3. Farewell dinner for Senior Accountant

Agenda items:
1. June 14 Electronics in production – detailed costings – JR
   June 21 Draft budget figures – JR

Research/drafts:
1. Memo of congratulations to N Div reps – via N Div Manager – soonest
2. Presentation speech – background on Senior Accountant

Reminders:
1. GB to telephone PK at home 8 June
2. JR to give GB preview of draft budget figs – asap but before 17 June

Check items off the original rough list as you draw up your action list by category. Check off each item on the action list when you initiate the necessary action and cross out each item when it has been completed or finalised.

Taking action

Diary: Settle the dates for the various meetings by telephoning those concerned. Confirm time, date and venue by memo for the director's/supervisors' meeting. Enter dates in your boss's diary as well as your own and draw his attention to the entries.

Agenda items: Note the agenda items in your diary on the days when you will be compiling the agenda, or put a note of them into the appropriate meeting file.

Research/drafts: The memo concerning the reps will go to their divisional manager. It should say why it is being written, include specific mention of how well the reps have done and should include the names of the reps concerned (see Fig 15). You will need to ask the Sales Director's secretary only for their names and to check what the figures are for their sales.

```
Re:  Recent sales results

I was very pleased to see that for the fourth consecutive week
Jim West, Gareth Mills and Trevor Jones have been more than
15% above their sales targets, with Gareth Mills achieving
+21% above budget last week. This is a splendid achievement,
particularly in the present economic state of the country.
                                   will have helped, but it is hard
Our advertising campaign in the north has more than justified   work & initiative
its cost by this considerable increase in sales and, I am as    in the field
pleased as you must be to see things going so consistently well. that gets
                                                                 this sort of
Congratulations to you and your team.                            result.
```

Fig 15 Draft memorandum

Your boss has improved this memo by his alterations – but your drafting of it in the first place has saved his time and given him a starting point.

For the draft speech of presentation, you will need to establish a few personal facts about the man who is leaving – what gifts are being presented and so on. His immediate boss, the Financial Director, and possibly the Personnel Officer, will be able to help with this. The draft you will provide for your boss here is intended only to give him a framework for his speech; not the finished product (see Fig 16).

Apart from the correction of 'proposing this toast' to 'making this presentation' the additions your boss has made are personal ones – his recollections – and though they may appear a bit sentimental or 'over the top' to you they are obviously right for this occasion. In drafting the 'bread and butter' part of the speech you have given your boss a base to build on, which is all he needed.

> ~~making His presentation~~
> I have mixed feelings in ~~proposing this toast~~ to Bob Henry.
> He has been such a pillar of strength to the firm for so
> long - 32 years last January.* ~~and~~ His good sense, meticulous
> attention to detail and never failing sense of humour have
> sustained us all in many a time of difficulty. He will
> leave a gap that will be impossible to fill and so I feel a
> sense of sadness at his departure. On the other hand, he and
> his wife Jenny are doing the only sensible thing; retiring
> early to a warmer and more healthy climate in Marbella - and
> I certainly envy them that!
>
> I want to thank them both for their help to the company - both
> in its early days when Jenny worked here too, and throughout
> the years as we grew. - *& they & their family grew too!*
>
> I have great pleasure in presenting ~~them~~ *Bob & Jenny* with our cheque and
> a gift of patio furniture - already waiting for them in
> Marbella - and to wish Bob many more years of happiness and
> improved health which I am sure he will achieve with the able
> and loving help of Jenny.
>
> *insert* * *12 years before I came to the company myself as Sales Manager. I remember well how he helped me in setting up what was in those days thought a 'revolutionary system' of sales accounting! He was then, as he has always been, a Company man - never parochial, never self interested. It has been the company's good fortune that he has worked with us and for us for so long.*

Fig 16 Draft presentation speech

From the revised speech you can now provide your boss with a series of small cards with a few words on each which will act as reminders at the presentation and enable him to give an 'impromptu' speech (see Fig 17).

```
MIXED FEELINGS

PILLAR OF STRENGTH - 32 years last Jan

12 YEARS BEFORE I JOINED

HELP IN 'REVOLUTIONARY SYSTEM'

TRUE 'COMPANY MAN'
```

Fig 17 Speech card

Reminders: Type a note reminding your boss to ring Peter King (include his home telephone number as he should receive the call at home on an occasion like this) and take it in with the incoming mail the next day.

Make a note in your diary to remind John Routh on 16 June if he has not contacted the MD by then to discuss the figures.

After dealing with the aftermath of this weekly meeting, together with your other work and possibly attendance at other meetings, it will probably be time to prepare and circulate the agenda for the meeting to be held on the 14th!

Summary

- Try to have at least two alternative dates for a proposed meeting; find out from your boss the names of those who *must* attend and telephone them first
- Prepare the meeting room in advance with everything necessary to assist those attending – and clear away promptly afterwards
- Make sure that *all* the required papers are in the meeting file in the correct order
- When preparing the agenda, enter the name of the person dealing with each item if appropriate; note on the chairman's agenda any items he particularly wants to mention
- Do not comment during a meeting unless invited to do so
- Take particular note of any items agreed upon and who is to be responsible for any forthcoming action
- Type the first draft of your notes as soon as possible after the meeting closes – preferably the same day
- Circulate the finished minutes or notes as soon as possible after the meeting date and certainly not more than a week later
- Draw the attention of those who have agreed to action items by highlighting the parts of the minutes which concern them
- Make yourself an 'action list' when transcribing your notes for your first draft – and take the necessary action
- Follow up before the next meeting on action indicated for others

7 Travel

Arranging and rearranging

In making arrangements for your boss to travel you need to know:

a where, when and how he intends to go
b why he is going, who and what he needs to see, and what he needs to take

Where, when and how

Once you know the answers to these questions, contact the clerk or section of your company responsible for travel arrangements. If there is no such facility, ring your local travel agent. At the first opportunity after starting a new job (and if your boss travels quite often) visit the travel agent and make yourself known to the person who is going to deal with your requests in the future. The friendly help of the travel agent is a resource to be nurtured. Don't spend your time learning railway timetables or airline schedules by heart. It is the travel agent's job to know the best (and the cheapest) way of getting from A to B via X and back again, so take advantage of his expertise. Tell him when your boss has to be in a certain place and for how long, the method of travel required, and leave the rest to the agent. Dealing with the answers to *b* will give you plenty to arrange on your own!

Foreign visits
If your boss is going abroad, make sure that his passport is in order and that he has the necessary visas and health documents where applicable. Telephone or telex the appropriate embassy or legation to ask what is required by their authorities and how to obtain it. Find out if comphrehensive insurance is arranged to cover accidents, illness, loss of money and belongings. If this is not covered by a company or personal insurance policy, organise separate temporary cover for the duration of the trip. Your travel agent or bank will arrange this for you.

If your boss is taking a car, contact the AA or RAC to find out and obtain whatever documentation and insurance he will be required to carry in the countries he is to visit.

Make sure you know of any public holidays or celebrations taking place in countries your boss is to visit so that his arrangements will not coincide with any close-down of business in those areas.

Accommodation and onward transport

Your boss may specify a particular hotel but, if he does not, find out how much the company is prepared to pay for accommodation and consult one of the many hotel guides available. There are agencies who offer a hotel booking service or, again, your travel agent may be able to help you. If you write, Telex or telephone direct, make sure there is a copy of the confirmation of the booking in the file that your boss will take with him. If he is attending a conference or seminar, hotel arrangements are often made by the conference secretary – but make sure that they have been taken care of just in case this service has not been included.

If the journey is to be by air, arrangements for transport to and from the airports at each stage of the journey will need to be made. When he is visiting a subsidiary or division of the company you can include a request to a secretary working in that division, who has local knowledge, for transport and hotel bookings when you arrange your boss's meetings.

Why, who and what

Your boss may be going to buy, sell, interview prospective agents or employees or to visit other divisions or subsidiaries of the company for meetings; he may be attending a conference or seminar or investigating a potential market. Find out from him all the reasons for his visit and ask him what papers he will want to take with him and who he will need to see.

If he is on a selling trip abroad and will be carrying samples, find out the customs regulations for the UK and for those countries he will be visiting. HM Customs Officers will be glad to help with your queries and to provide, or tell you where to obtain, the necessary forms for completion.

Currency

Find out how much money your boss wants to take with him and arrange with the bank for travellers' cheques and foreign currency to be provided in good time. Make sure you remind your boss to take his passport to the bank when collecting the currency if restrictions are in force. Bear in mind that currency restrictions change.

Your boss will need to visit the bank himself to collect his travellers' cheques as each has to be signed by the user in the presence of a bank official. If the collection of cheques and currency has to be done some time in advance, ensure that these are securely locked away in the company safe until needed for the journey.

Make a travel checklist for yourself (see Figs 18 and 19) and an itinerary for your boss (see Fig 20 on page 102). The checklist can be photocopied for use on future trips and you simply tick each item as requested, and then as completed. Have a specific 'visit' file or folder ready to receive each document as it comes to you.

```
Visit to:
Dates:
Purpose:

                                        Requested    Completed

Tickets/reservation slips
Money/credit cards
Accommodation
Transport to & from station/airport

Meetings:  names/times/papers/samples
Itinerary/diary
```

Fig 18 Checklist for visits in the UK

```
Visit to:
Dates:
Purpose:

                                        Requested    Completed

Passport
Visas
Health documents
Insurance (personal & product)
Customs documentation
Tickets/reservation slips
Money:  cash
        traveller's cheques
        credit cards
Transport to & from air/seaport
Accommodation:  reservation documents
Meetings:  names/times/papers/samples
Itinerary/diary
```

Fig 19 Checklist for visits abroad

Visit to:		Paris and Bordeaux
Dates:		July 6 to 9 inclusive
Purpose:		Regular visit to subsidiary (Charles Cartier & Fils) + Paris Air Show.
DATE & TIME		
July 6	0800	Car from home to London Heathrow (Hire company D H Jones telephone: 01 772 000)
	0830	Check in at British Airways desk - Flight BA100
	0900	BA100 departs for Paris (Orly)
	1100 (local time)	Arrive Orly Airport
		Car from Cartier & Fils to collect
	1200	Arrive Cartier & Fils, Bld St Germaine
		Meetings and lunch with M Charles & M Henri Cartier
	afternoon:	Meetings
	evening:	Car (Cartier's) to collect from office and take to HOTEL ST GEORGE (address, telephone and telex no) and wait to take to dinner with M & Mme Charles Cartier and return to hotel
July 7	0830	M Henri Cartier to collect for whole day's visit to Paris Air Show (Henri Cartier's home telephone no)
	night	HOTEL ST GEORGE (confirm taxi for 0730 tommorrow)
July 8	0730	Taxi to Gare de Lyons
	0750	Train to Bordeaux
	1130	Arrive Bordeaux (M Yves Cartier to meet)
		Visits to factories
	night	Dinner and overnight stay with M & Mme Yves Cartier (address and telephone no)
July 9	1145	Car to Bordeaux - Merignac Airport
	1230	Check in at Air France desk - Flight AF212 to London Heathrow
	1300 (local time)	Arrive Heathrow
		Car from office to meet (Tom Watts driver)
	1400	Arrive office
	1630	Meeting with executive directors

Fig 20 Example of an itinerary

Before your boss leaves, find the time to discuss with him what is likely to happen in the office while he is away and how he wants you to deal with things. Try to arrange with him times when he will telephone so that urgent matters can be covered.

Rearrangements

Very often plans you and your travel agent have spent a great deal of time and effort in arranging to perfection will have to be changed. Sometimes they will need to be changed more than once. With your checklists to hand these rearrangements are not difficult – just time consuming. With the travel agent on your side your task is considerably lightened; goodwill can ease many an irritating situation. Be tolerant – these rearrangements are not normally just your boss's whim, but have genuine reasons behind them. Pay meticulous attention to every detail when you rearrange a trip and make sure that all who need to know of the changes are informed as soon as possible.

Itineraries and checklists

Obviously you will adapt your style of itinerary preparation to what your boss requires. He will tell you what he wants included and to whom copies should be given. On his own copy he may want to add more detailed personal summaries of what he should be doing, buying or collecting. For example, his wife or family may have asked him to purchase something for them or he may want to bring gifts back with him.

It is possible that he will not want you to type a specific itinerary at all and will simply accept the one provided by the travel agent, using his pocket diary to note the extra times and dates for meetings etc. In any event, make sure all diaries are completed with all the details needed.

After your boss departs

While your boss is away you will be able to catch up with all your non-priority jobs (probably the tedious ones you have managed to put off for weeks), improve any systems you have found not to be working well and get any maintenance jobs done in his office. If he is to be away for more than a few days, deal with his incoming post either by passing a copy to the appropriate deputy (keeping the original and noting what action was taken by the deputy) or, if the matter can be dealt with only by your boss, by writing a short note explaining the delay to the writer. If urgent action must be taken by your boss, then you will have to contact him by telephone or Telex to ask for his instructions.

Keep folders for all his incoming mail (and copies of your replies), sorted into batches of important and urgent items which need action; items on which action has already been taken; reports or memoranda of interest or potential interest; magazines and periodicals in which you have marked articles he might care to read.

On his return

Have a shortlist of urgent items for his immediate attention and reserve all non-essentials for your next meeting. He will probably have either tapes or notes of his various meetings for you to deal with as soon as possible and anything other than first priority work from you will not be welcome.

'... anything other than first priority work will not be welcome.'

When you first see him after his return, make sure that you obtain from him all the documents relating to insurance, customs, etc that you need, the balance of his travellers' cheques and cash (in the unlikely event that he has any left!), copies of receipts for expenses and the papers he took away with him (if they were originals and not just extra copies).

Travelling for your company

There are situations where you will be asked to travel with, or even instead of, your boss. The latter is rare, since if he is prevented from making the trip himself, it is more usual for his deputy or another executive with appropriate knowledge to stand in for him. However, it can happen that you are the executive best qualified to deputise, and if so there are a few general points to keep in mind.

The research and preparatory work you do will be precisely what you would have done if your boss were going alone. If you accompany him, give the same supportive aid you give when in your office. If you deputise, take especial care to find out what he will want to know and keep accurate and comprehensive notes to present to him on your return. At all times you should be your usual efficient and helpful self and keep in mind that a business trip is not a holiday – it is simply working away from home base. Listen more than you talk; remember that you are your boss's and your company's representative and behave accordingly.

Should the visit be to a conference or meeting, ensure that you bring back with you all the printed information issued and write your notes as soon as possible afterwards so that you can present your report quickly. In the rather unlikely event that you are to stand in for your boss as a speaker at either meeting or conference, you will be working from his prepared lecture or speech and will preface your performance by explaining why you are there and he is not. If you and he have compiled the paper together mainly from your research, you will be able to handle a question session. If not, and you really do not know the subject well, make sure you explain this too before reading the paper.

Clothes

If you are to travel by air, make sure that you travel light. If you can, pack all you need in a case which will be allowed as cabin baggage; you will save yourself a lot of time by not having to wait for the luggage to be unloaded and claimed. When your destination is abroad you will be able to go straight through to customs and immigration control at your arrival point. Take clothes that do not need pressing – and don't take too many of them. Your wardrobe will probably contain a number of items that mix and match and by various permutations you will manage to survive. Remember that men seldom travel with more than one suit (other than the one they are wearing) and sufficient changes of underwear, socks and shirts for the length of their stay. It is quite possible for you to do likewise, with the addition of one elegant – and lightweight – outfit for the lucky occasion when you are asked out to dine in the city's most exclusive restaurant!

'... make sure that you travel light.'

Language

If you travel to countries where English is not commonly understood, it is well worth learning at least one foreign language. Speaking another language – French and German particularly – is becoming more and more important in business and can be of enormous use to you and your firm, even if you rarely or never travel abroad. Your company may feel that your representing them merits their investing in a language laboratory course for you, but even if they do not, there are a number of record/cassette and textbook courses available for you to teach yourself. If you have to make a journey abroad and do not speak that country's language, at least familiarise yourself with a few commonly used words and phrases, and take a phrase book and dictionary with you. This is not only helpful to you but courteous to your host country. If you can speak French or German as well as English you will probably find that you can make yourself understood in, say, Greece or Hungary or Spain, but a few words in Greek or Hungarian or Spanish as well make a very good impression.

Attitude

While you are away remember always that you are representing your firm – and, if abroad, your country – so everything you do reflects upon them. If you have lived or spent your holidays abroad, you will know that being relaxed and being your own polite self is all that is necessary to be a successful ambassador. If you are to travel abroad for the first time on a business trip, however, it may be difficult for you to be relaxed or even to be yourself! The qualities you need to succeed at home – tolerance, attention and courtesy to other people and a sense of humour, for example – will be needed abroad in rather larger measure. Avoid being overbearing and critical at all costs. The maxim 'when in Rome. . .' has a lot to recommend it. If you accept the differences between 'us' and 'them' and appreciate the good things you find rather than criticising the bad, you will stand more chance of doing successfully the job you have been sent to do; you will make useful contacts for your firm, friends for yourself and enjoy the whole experience.

Summary

- Make sure of the purpose of the trip; the answers to where, why, who and what
- Draw up the appropriate checklist and work from it
- Collaborate with your travel agent – use all the services available
- Write the itinerary and mark up the diaries
- Ensure all necessary papers are in order and taken on the trip
- Deal only with essential and urgent matters when your boss first returns – take work from him rather than giving work to him
- If you travel for your company remember to travel light; take the trouble to learn the language; tolerate and respect differences

8 Advancement

Deciding when to move on

Once a job becomes mere routine and week after week passes without a challenge to your initiative – and never a rush of adrenalin – then it is time to ask yourself the question 'Am I ready to settle for comfort, security, boredom and a running-down process?' If the answer is 'no', then it is time to move on.

If you work for a really large or multinational company and if you are not in the top secretarial position already, there will probably be opportunities to progress within your company. Discuss your feelings and ambitions with your boss and with the Personnel Officer; make it clear that you need to grow – to move on and up – and that if possible you would like to do so within the company. If there is no chance (possibly because the top secretariat is firmly ensconced with no one there wanting to move on for some time) then you must start on the process of searching elsewhere (and go back to Chapter 3 again).

Make the decision to move on before you have become so bored with your job that you have let your abilities and enthusiasm deteriorate. Unless you have experienced a truly 'growing' job where you have gained more and more responsibility (and in some places, however good you are and however hard you try, you will not have been given the extra responsibility you know you could handle), you will probably get the 'moving on' urge every two to five years. As in gambling, the maxim 'quit while you're ahead' applies. Don't stay at the tables in the belief that your luck will change or in a job in the hope that things must improve. Use your judgment and knowledge of the environment and, once you are convinced that nothing you can do will change your role to extend your abilities, make your plans for moving.

Moving on with style

Tell your boss of your intention to look for another job before you start doing so and explain why you want to leave. (He will probably be aware anyway that you have outgrown the challenges the job can offer.) Make sure that you leave him with a replacement who will continue to give him excellent secretarial support. It must always be a temptation to want to be missed; to have a replacement who does not do everything as well as you have done it, and to want to be thought indispensable. Don't succumb to this temptation; making sure that things run just as smoothly after you leave is one more proof of your outstanding abilities.

It is not difficult, having run an efficient office, to make sure that your successor can do likewise. Since you have never kept information only in your head (because you recognised that there would be times when you would not be available to dispense it), your files and records are up to date and clearly defined. The tasks you regularly perform are indicated on your job description (which you have up-dated as your responsibilities have grown). When you decide to leave, look through this description again carefully, as though you were just beginning in the job and ask yourself if every task is sufficiently well explained to be easily understood by a newcomer.

Put together a file of examples of the regular tasks you undertake and staple to each of the examples a written outline of the routine you follow – the timescale for completion, names of people concerned in that routine who can be asked for assistance if needed, and a simple background on the purpose of the task. Type notes on the procedure for meetings and ensure that circulation lists give the full names of everyone concerned, not just their initials. Write a glossary of of the shortforms or venacular terms generally in use in your firm. (This applies especially in the Civil or Public Service where so many committees and departments are known and referred to *only* by their initial letters.) Make sure the organisation chart is current. Find your original 'portraits' of your boss's colleagues and see if there is anything you can add or change that will be helpful.

Give very careful thought to what a newcomer will need to know in order not to be overwhelmed by what to you has become second-nature. It should be possible for someone to take over from you without having an overlap period, but if you find a suitable replacement prepared to start working with you a week or so before you leave, so much the better for a smooth handover. You will be able to introduce her to the people she needs to know and be available to answer her questions.

Do not tell her *how* to perform each task. Provide her with the background information needed, why jobs have to be done and when, and let her do them in her own way. We are all different in our approach and you cannot leave a carbon copy of yourself behind. If you and your boss have chosen the right person, she will be sure to give as good a service as you have – but in her own way. You may find that you can learn from her too and will be able to bring a new approach to tasks in your next job. Unless your company has been in a constant state of flux and growth while you have been with them, it is more than likely that you have not brought many fresh views to the job for some time and a change will benefit not only you, but the boss and company you are leaving as well.

'. . . you cannot leave a carbon copy of yourself behind.'

If your replacement starts before you leave, you will have time to say your farewells and thanks to those who have worked with you and helped you during your stay, and still be available as an information resource to your successor. Never pass on your prejudices or preferences for individuals to the one who takes over your job. Simply because Mr Jones in Accounts has been a thorn in your flesh for years does not mean that he will not be a complete charmer to the 'new girl'. Don't make the mistake of telling Mr Jones precisely what you think of him. It may have appealed to your imagination in moments of conflict with him in the past, but it will do no one any good, least of all yourself. After all, you never know how, when and in what circumstances you may meet again!

Summary

- Once you are sure you can no longer grow in a job, make plans for leaving
- Tell your boss of your intention to leave before you start looking for something else

- Ensure that everything can run as smoothly after you leave as it did while you were there; this is another proof of your quality
- Look at the tasks you perform from the viewpoint of a newcomer, and explain them in writing accordingly
- Tell your successor what has to be done and why, but not precisely how to do it; her approach and personality will not necessarily be anything like yours
- Never pass on your prejudices or preferences for individuals
- Always say goodbye and thank you to those who have worked with you, and *never* tell those with whom you have had difficulties just what you think of them!

So ... you have engaged a replacement and she is happily starting on a new stage in her career – with all the help you could possibly give her to make a success of it. And you have found just the job you want; another company, perhaps even another town or country and the opportunity to start a new way of life. You will be ready to play a different role with renewed enthusiasm to meet whatever challenge it can give.

Good luck!